C

01-76(

GW01079967

A GUIDE TO

JAZZ, FOLK and AUSTRALIAN MUSIC

A GUIDE TO

JAZZ, FOLK and AUSTRALIAN MUSIC

Peter Dunbar-Hall · Glenda Hodge

S

Science Press

Science Press
Fitzroy and Chapel Streets
Marrickville NSW 2204

© Science Press 1991

First published 1991

National Library of Australia
Cataloguing-in-Publication data

Dunbar-Hall, P. (Peter).
    A guide to jazz, folk and Australian music.

    ISBN 0 85583 178 2.

    1. Jazz music — History and criticism — Juvenile
    literature. 2. Folk music — History and criticism —
    Juvenile literature. 3. Music — Australia — History and
    criticism — Juvenile literature. I. Hodge, G. (Glenda).
    II Title.

780.9

Cover Photograph
Kate Ceberano, winner of the Australian Record Industries Award
for best Australian Female Artist of the Year for 1988 and 1989.
Reproduced by kind permission of Kate Ceberano Productions and
Mr Fred Bray, photographer.

Design by Frances Barty

Set in 11/11pt. Baskerville

Printed in Singapore.

Contents

Preface

A Guide to Jazz, Folk and Australian Music is a companion volume to the authors' successful *Guide to Rock and Pop*. It treats three important areas of music study by historical discussion, examination of musical elements, and inclusion of many pieces of music for classroom performance and analysis.

As with all the books by Glenda Hodge and Peter Dunbar-Hall, this new title includes worksheets, listening lists, and follow-up activities to the work. The range of learning methods covers the syllabus areas of aural perception, creative work, practical experience and background research.

JAZZ

The Background of Jazz

No one knows for certain where the word 'jazz' originally came from or what it initially meant. What we do know is that it came to be used to refer to a type of music that developed among Negroes during the last quarter of the 19th century in the southern states of America. It was an eclectic style, combining elements from African music, ragtime, spirituals, marches, and blues.

AFRICAN MUSIC

When the slave traders took Africans from the coast of West Africa to America, the slaves carried their cultures with them in the form of songs, dances, languages and dialects. Although at times the white slave owners tried to stop the slaves singing and dancing their atavistic music, the traditions survived, sometimes purely for enjoyment, sometimes for subversive purposes. It is natural then that the songs and dances brought over from Africa could influence later developments in music among the Negro slaves although the slaves themselves, being born in America, might have no physical links with Africa.

Two important musical elements of jazz can be seen in songs from Africa. Often these songs are constructed from a series of questions and answers (also called **call and response**). If you listen to some examples of early jazz you will hear this same device being used between the instruments of the group. Second, African music is usually **pentatonic**, that is, it uses only five notes. This characteristic was carried over into blues songs and via the blues scale into jazz, so quite often the melodic lines of jazz are influenced by pentatonic music.

Another important general influence of African music on jazz is that of rhythm. African music uses many percussion instruments, and rhythmic devices such as **polyrhythm** and **cross rhythm** are very important. One of the most prominent elements of jazz is its feel for rhythm — the percussive sounds, and the often irregular and complex rhythms could be traced back to African music.

RAGTIME

This type of popular piano music flourished in the last quarter of the 19th century among black pianists. It was played in bars, gambling dens and brothels, and although today we think of only one man, Scott Joplin (1868–1917), as a ragtime composer, it was very popular and was written by many other people. The name of the style (again we are not sure what it means) may refer to the intense syncopation of the music which is very **ragged**. This is in fact its main musical characteristic, and the element it contributed to jazz.

Look at the musical example of ragtime, better still play it, and notice the syncopation of the right hand against the march-like rhythm of the left hand (= cross rhythm). This example by

1

its title helps us remember the importance of syncopation, and from its copyright date (1902), when this style was popular.

ELITE SYNCOPATION

Not fast.

By Scott Joplin

3

This style of left hand playing is known as **stride** playing; it is very rhythmical and is the style used by pianists in New Orleans style jazz as well. It is possibly another example of the influence of ragtime on early jazz.

SPIRITUALS

Spirituals are religious songs sung by Negroes. Usually the words of spirituals refer to the salvation of death, and often by Biblical allusion equate the plight of the Negro slaves with the captivity of the Jews in the Old Testament. Musically, spirituals are often pentatonic (a carry over from African music) and use the call and response pattern, for example,

As far as influence on jazz is concerned, many famous jazz standards are instrumental versions of spirituals; the call and response idea is found in jazz; and the instrumental techniques of jazz, especially early jazz, try to imitate the vocal style of Negro songs, including spirituals.

MARCHES

Military music could be heard in all the American states in the latter half of the 19th century, especially during the American Civil War (1861–1865). After the war was over many of the army bands were disbanded and instruments were sold off or pawned, to be bought by Negro musicians. This explains why the instrumentation of early jazz groups includes clarinet, cornet, trombone, and tuba. Apart from this, march music also contributed its four-square beat, which can be heard in early jazz, and its use of simple European harmony based on the primary triads of major keys (that is, chords I, IV, and V). The importance of a strong bass line that picks out the underlying harmonic pattern could also be an influence of military music on jazz.

BATTLE HYMN OF THE REPUBLIC

Melody — "John Brown's Body"
Words — Julia Ward Howe

2. In the beauty of the lilies Christ was born across the sea,
   With a glory in His bosom that transfigures you and me.
   As He died to make men holy let us die to make men free,
   His truth is marching on.
   Glory, glory, etc.

BLUES

The blues are a special repertoire of songs belonging to the Negro slaves. They are a distinct form of folk poetry with strong sociological importance. They lament the condition of slavery, or are about unhappy love affairs. Often they mention suicide and death. The lyrics of the most common form of blues consist of three lines of which the first two are the same, and the third is a summing up or conclusion of the thoughts in the first two. The music consists of three four-bar phrases, usually the first two are the same. Under the melody is the 12 bar blues chord sequence, for example,

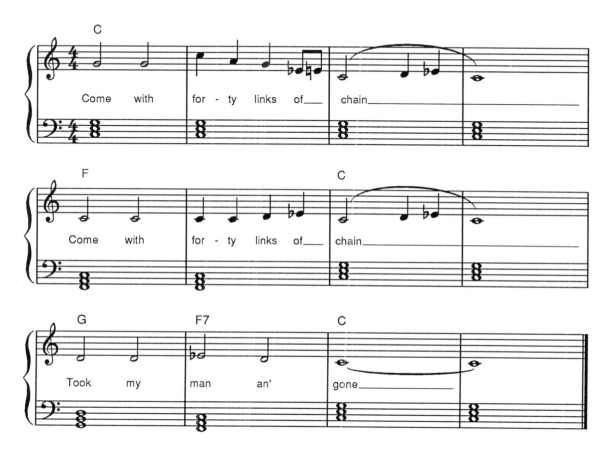

It is from these songs that jazz receives its most important musical elements — harmony, melody, and formal structure.

Harmonically, early jazz and the subsequent styles rely heavily on the 12 bar blues. Melodically, many jazz numbers are instrumental versions of blues songs. Formally, much jazz simply copies the repetition of the 12 bar pattern just as in blues songs.

Another influence of blues on jazz can be found in the instrumental style which tries to imitate the vocal effects of blues singers. This explains the slide effects of trombone parts, and also the use of **blue notes**. Blue notes are chromatic notes that don't fit into the harmony. They help create the blues effect of jazz. The melodic character of blues and jazz relies on these notes which can be seen in the blues scale. There are different versions of what constitutes a blues scale, usually relating to how many notes there should be. Some have only five showing a direct link with the melodies of some African songs, others have the missing notes filled in. The common factor in all versions is the flattened third, which creates a clash when played or sung over the chords of a 12 bar blues sequence,

9

In performance a blue note is sometimes followed by the neighbouring semitone which does fit the harmony,

One of the results of using the flattened third degree of a scale is that if it is played over the fifth and sixth bars of a 12 bar sequence,

the resulting sound is based on a minor seventh chord,

This could be how harmonic vocabulary is extended and why the blues sound so logical if they are played with all seventh chords.

Revision questions

Explain each of the following musical terms, and say for each one which type of music it comes from — African music, ragtime, spirituals, marches, blues.

1. question and answer

2. pentatonic

3. cross rhythm

4. syncopation

5. stride playing

6. call and response

7. primary triads, I, IV, and V

8. blues

9. 12 bar blues

10. blue notes

(For answers, see page 127.)

Activities

Listen to and perform other examples of these types of music. When you have learnt to recognise the musical elements and characteristics discussed in this section complete the following worksheet.

Worksheet 1

Listen to some examples of early jazz, identify the elements in the examples that are related to the styles discussed in this section, and fill in the necessary information below.

Title of music	
Performer/s	**Date**
Musical element	**Link to previous style**

History of Jazz Styles

The development of jazz can be divided into roughly 10-year sections. This is not to say that every decade a new style took over completely, rather, a new style seemed to emerge and overlap the older styles but all progressed along together. Because jazz developed at the time of the discovery of sound recording and the record-making process, many examples of jazz recorded earlier this century are available. This has allowed each style to maintain its uniqueness and integrity, with all styles remaining popular today.

1890s

Jazz as we know it is generally said to have begun in the last decade of the 19th century and the first decade of this century. There were several styles of music that are often considered as jazz, however they are precursors of jazz and predate it by several years. Best known of these are blues and ragtime.

Ragtime is composed music written for solo piano. There is no improvisation but its feel is that of jazz (that is, it 'swings'). It takes its form from European music and is usually in several sections in succession like a Strauss waltz or Sousa march. World Fairs held around the country in the latter part of the 19th century — St Louis, Baltimore, Chicago — popularised the style with white audiences. Famous performers include:

Scott Joplin   **Tom Turpin**
James Scott   **Jelly Roll Morton**
Eubie Blake

The left hand style was developed throughout the 1920s, becoming known as 'stride' in the 1930s and 1940s. (See Instruments in Jazz — Piano)

1900s — NEW ORLEANS

Jazz was heard and played all over the south and mid-west of America (Kansas, Memphis, St Louis and Dallas) in the early years of this century. Jazz is said to have developed in New Orleans however, because until the 1930s, most of the important jazz performers came from there.

New Orleans was a bustling seaport where a mixture of races and cultures, with their varied musical traditions, came together. Europeans from England, France and Spain (Louisiana was bought from the French in 1803 with 'The Louisiana Purchase') coexisted with two strains of black African descendants.

The creoles, of mixed French and black parentage, were descendants of the slaves of the French who were freed much earlier than other blacks. They had a proud tradition, spoke a kind of French/English patois or dialect and had French names, like jazz musicians Sidney Bechet and Ferdinand Joseph Le Menthe (better known as Jelly Roll Morton). They kept French traditions like the mardi gras and funeral processions and played the clarinet as their main instrument (a favourite instrument of the European French). The American Negroes, on the other hand, had been freed more recently and were therefore much poorer. Their musical and cultural traditions were different to those of the creoles in that most of their influences came from their African inheritance.

The coming together of so many disparate musical ingredients sparked off the music we know as jazz. The red-light district of Storyville in New Orleans gave many musicians the opportunity of working in its brothels, bars and dance halls.

A typical New Orleans group consisted of a front line of cornet, trombone and clarinet. These instruments carried the melody. They were supported by a rhythm section consisting of a bass instrument (string or tuba), drums, banjo or guitar, and occasionally piano. New Orleans jazz variations closely resemble the original melody and the strong beats are on the

12

first and third beats of the bar (like a march). The harmonic pattern is the 12 bar blues and the style is described as **collective improvisation**. That is, everyone played the introduction and the first chorus (or pattern of chords), all improvising at the same time. Each player then took a turn at a solo improvisation and the piece ended with another group improvisation.

It is interesting to note that the great examples of New Orleans jazz (such as King Oliver's Creole Jazz Band and Louis Armstrong's Hot Five) were not recorded until the 1920s in Chicago.

Storyville, New Orleans

A traditional New Orleans jazz parade

Listening

1. New Orleans is often called a 'hot style' of playing. From your listening, what do you think this means?
2. What examples did you listen to? What instruments could you hear? Analyse the form and the order of solos.

1910 — DIXIELAND

Blacks of the south and mid-west were not the only people exposed to the contrasting musical elements which fostered the development of jazz. Whites also played in jazz bands and developed a white New Orleans jazz which we call Dixieland. The most well known of these white groups were the Original Dixieland Jazz Band and the New Orleans Rhythm Kings.

Though existing at the same time, Dixieland generally means white jazz while New Orleans jazz refers to the black version. The white style tended to be harmonically more correct, more technical, less expressive (today we might say less funky or played with less soul) and more orthodox in its sound. It used fewer black performance features such as sliding between notes, glissandi and vibrato and, unlike New Orleans jazz, rarely made use of solo improvisations.

It was these white Dixieland groups who first made jazz popular with white audiences. (In 1917, the Original Dixieland Jazz Band played to packed houses in New York.) Dixieland is one of the styles of jazz still popular today and can be heard the world over in parades, bars and hotels.

Listening

Listen to some Dixieland jazz and then complete the table.

Name of tune	Group	Instruments	Role of instruments

14

1920s — CHICAGO

Looking for work, many blacks left the depressed south around 1915 (WWI) and moved north to the big industrial cities of New York and Chicago. The closure of Storyville also hastened the northerly exodus of musicians, such as King Oliver and Louis Armstrong, who settled in the black south side of Chicago. With the transfer from the country town of New Orleans to the city, their music lost some of its exuberance and easy style, becoming slightly faster and more frenetic, reflecting the brashness of a busy city life.

On the other hand, this influx of talented black musicians influenced white performers and the first white jazz players came to prominence — including Benny Goodman (clarinet), Bix Beiderbecke (cornet) and Gene Krupa (drums). The white bands decided to use popular songs (in AABA form) rather than the traditional black 12 bar blues in their performances.

The recording industry, realising the potential of this new music, helped make jazz popular by recording many of the great performers of the age. The recordings of New Orleans jazz by Louis Armstrong and His Hot Five, King Oliver and Jelly Roll Morton (and His Red Hot Peppers) date from this time, as do the classic blues recordings of singers like Ma Rainey and Bessie Smith. (Though blues had been around for almost 100 years, it finally reached its heyday in the 1920s in Chicago.)

The role of the instrumental soloist increased in importance and an arrangement usually consisted of an opening ensemble, followed by a solo on each instrument, concluded by another ensemble playing.

Listening

Complete the table after listening to some examples of Chicago jazz.

Performing group	Name of song	Musical observations

Ella Fitzgerald

Louis Armstrong

1930s — SWING

In the 1930s, the centre of jazz moved from Chicago to New York, where the popularity of jazz as dance music continued to grow. Large dance halls, radio broadcasts and the 'movies' helped make the era of the big bands and the swing music they played one of the most popular styles in the history of jazz.

Bands became much larger and there was an emphasis on the three main sections in the band — trumpets, trombones and saxophones. With more members in a band there had to be less freedom in performance. Free improvisation was consequently discarded or at least written into the performance. Arrangements for so many musicians had to be made and written down as 'charts' for the performers to play. Performers needed to become musically literate (they had to be able to read the music written for them) and the bands became tightly disciplined groups. This was the era of the arranger — Duke Ellington, Count Basie and Fletcher Henderson among others. The best of these arrangers tried to keep the feel of jazz, while keeping the sound of the bands smooth and sophisticated. The music was in $\frac{4}{4}$ but with a slight emphasis on each beat. The use of riffs (short repeated melodic fragments) by trumpet, trombone and sax sections created excitement and gave the characteristic big band sound.

The movies helped spread the popularity of these swing bands and many of the band leaders are familiar even today.

Fletcher Henderson   **Dorsey Brothers**
Glenn Miller   **Duke Ellington**
Count Basie   **Jack Teagarden**
Artie Shaw   **Paul Whiteman**
Luis Russell

Though the swing bands had a group sound, the soloist in the band also had a vital role. Some of these soloists are as famous as the bands they played in; they include Coleman Hawkins (tenor sax), Benny Goodman (clarinet), Gene Krupa and Cozy Cole (drums), Johnny Hodges (alto sax), and Fats Waller (piano).

Many legendary jazz singers had their beginnings singing in these bands — Billie Holiday, Ella Fitzgerald, Ethel Waters and Mildred Bailey, to name a few.

The Benny Goodman Orchestra

STORMY WEATHER

Music by Harold Arlen
Words by Ted Koehler

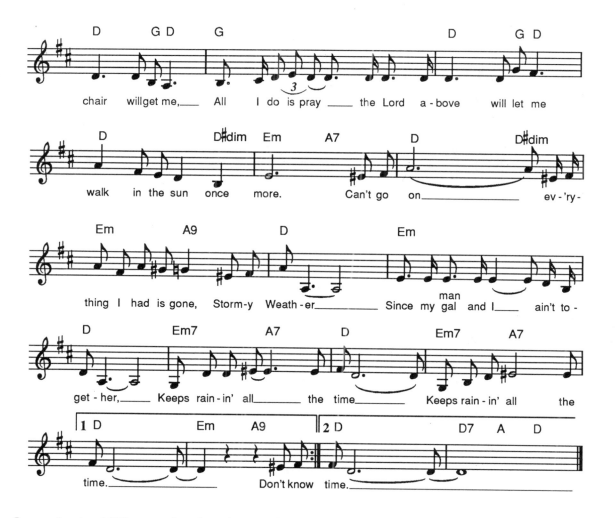

It was in the 1930s too, that boogie-woogie developed as a popular piano style. Based on the 12 bar blues, it probably developed around 1920 but it reached its height of popularity in the 1930s. Its distinctive sound is centred around the driving left hand dotted rhythm patterns (♪♪) known as '8 to a bar'. These can be of several types (see page 57) while the right hand plays melodic variations on 12 bar blues harmonies. Performers in this style include:

Meade 'Lux' Lewis   Albert Ammons
Clarence 'Pinetops' Smith   Pete Johnson
Jimmy Yancey

''Tuxedo Junction'' was made popular by Glenn Miller's band in the 1930s and early 1940s. It is arranged here for voices. You might like to double the vocal line on instruments.

19

TUXEDO JUNCTION

By Buddy Feyne, Erskin Hawkins, William Johnson and Julian Dash

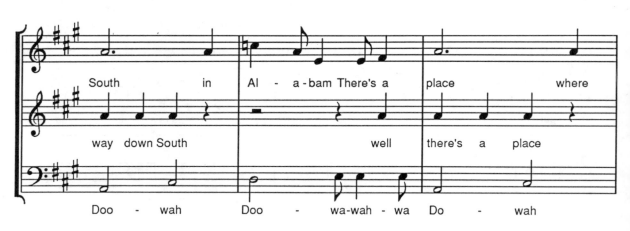

Questions

1. What key is the song in?
2. What is the name for the repeated note in the second part?
3. What is the term used for describing the 'nonsense' syllables in the bass line?
4. Circle four bars that use syncopation.
5. What is syncopation?
6. Complete this table of musical signs used in the song.

Sign	Meaning
𝄐	
♮	
𝄬	

(For answers, see page 127.)

This song was made popular during the big band era by the Andrews Sisters who sang it in close harmony much like it is written here. You might like to play it on xylophones or glockenspiels while you sing.

RUM AND COCA COLA

By M. Amsterdam, J. Sullivan and P. Baron

If you ev - er go to Trin - i - dad they make you feel so ve - ry glad Ca-

lyp - so sing and make up rhyme guar-an - tee you one good real fine time. Drink-in'

Rum and Co - ca_____ Co - la   Go down Point Koo - ma - nah

Both mo-ther and___ daugh-ter   Work - ing for the   Yan - kee dol - lar___

Questions

1. What form is this song in?
2. Circle two examples of syncopation in the song.
3. What is the time signature? Put it in at the beginning of the music.
4. What key is the song in?
5. Write out the scale and the two chords that harmonise the song.

(For answers, see page 128.)

Listening

Boogie

Performer	Name of piece	Style of left hand playing	Musical observations (tempo, virtuosity, melody etc)

Swing

Name of band	Name of piece	Melodic observations (instrumental groups heard, solos etc)

1940s (and 1950s) — BEBOP

World War II marked the end of the swing period. Though it was still very popular with audiences, many of the performers enlisted to fight, others longed for the freedom to return to improvised jazz or rebelled against the commercialisation of the style.

Whatever the reason, a new style of jazz emerged in New York during the 1940s. At its centre was a small group of performers who were technically brilliant and able to improvise around new and complex harmonies. The melodies and improvisations were often very fast and musically sophisticated. Short melodic fragments were put together in a nervous, frenetic way, often using the dissonances characteristic of the times. Bebop (later bop) got its onomatopoeic name from the sound of the interval of a flattened fifth, a favoured interval of the bebop musicians.

Some of the most famous performers of the era include:

Thelonius Monk (piano, double bass)　　**Lenny Tristano, Bud Powell (piano)**
Miles Davis, Dizzy Gillespie (trumpet)　　**Kenny Clarke (drums)**
Charlie Parker, Lester Young (saxophone)　**Charlie Christian (guitar)**

Many of these black bebop artists went to live and work in France to escape from racial discrimination and prejudice in their own country. They began the great love of jazz held by Europeans. One of the principal jazz festivals in the world is held at Montreux in Switzerland.

As a reaction to this style, many whites returned to the traditional or Dixieland jazz. This 'trad' jazz is still popular, though the sounds of bebop today are just as familiar.

Listening

1. Listen to an example of bebop. How is it different to the sounds of earlier jazz?
2. Research the life of a bebop composer. What did you listen to of this composer?

Dizzy Gillespie

1950s — COOL AND HARD BOP

The nervous energy that characterised bebop of the 1940s gave way to a much calmer, smoother, more intellectual and less emotional style of music in the 1950s. Cool jazz, as it was known, was introduced by Miles Davis, a trumpeter who had played with Charlie Parker and Dizzy Gillespie in the 1940s; John Lewis and Lennie Tristano, pianists; and Tadd Dameron, arranger.

An important sound of cool jazz is that of the vibraphone which had been used in jazz since the 1930s but became very popular in the 1950s with players such as Lionel Hampton and Milt Jackson.

On the west coast of America, jazz musicians who had found work in the recording and movie industries played a style of cool jazz that rivalled the popularity of jazz in the eastern states. Dave Brubeck is probably the best known of the West Coast Cool School.

Bop refined itself into 'hard bop', a musical style requiring great technical ability, as well as a profound knowledge of complex harmonies and how to improvise around them.

Performers include:

Max Roach, Art Blakey (drums)
Horace Silver (piano)

Clifford Brown (trumpet)
Sonny Rollins, John Coltrane (saxophone)

1960s — FREE JAZZ

Jazz in the 1960s entered into an experimental period. Performers looked for new ideas in an attempt to free themselves from what they felt were jazz clichés. They adapted many ideas and harmonic schemes (such as atonality, 12 tone and serial techniques), from avant-garde European composers and the music from other cultures, especially Africa, India and Arabia, provided the inspiration for rhythmic variation (such as doing away with the reliance on a regular beat and meter).

Like other 20th century composers, jazz musicians investigated the whole range of sounds their instruments could make in an attempt to make their music as free and spontaneous as

Miles Davis

Keith Jarrett

possible. Ornette Coleman, John Coltrane, Charles Mingus, Miles Davis and Keith Jarrett were the central figures in this style.

Third stream jazz was an attempt in the 1960s to blend classical music and jazz. The result of the merging of these two streams, one structured, the other improvised, is the third stream.

Latin and South American influences were also important in this period. Although North and South America shared similar black cultural roots (as slaves had been taken from Africa to both areas), the music of South America had developed along different lines and had a different sound to that of North American jazz.

In the 1960s, the instruments of Latin and South America such as congas, cowbells, rattles, guiros and claves, together with many of their rhythms (like the samba) were fused with jazz to produce improvised music with a completely different sound and feel. A famous example of this is the bossa nova, 'The Girl from Iparena'.

1970s — MODERN JAZZ AND ELECTRIC

Rock 'n' roll began in the 1950s with a combining of jazz, country and western, and blues elements. By the 1970s rock had repaid the debt, influencing jazz among other styles. Miles Davis with the record *Bitches Brew* (1970) heralded this new style which was called fusion (or jazz rock fusion).

Fusion takes the basic rock rhythm section of guitars and drums and adds jazz elements, principally horns (brass and saxophones) and keyboards. Riffs on horns are taken from jazz and the harmonies are much more complex than basic rock. The instruments of fusion are usually electric. Apart from electric pianos and guitars, the brass and reed instruments are often amplified by means of attached pick-ups. Synthesisers are utilised to expand the range of sounds.

Fusion groups include Blood Sweat and Tears, Chicago, Weather Report, and Mahavishnu Orchestra.

Some jazz composers, like Herbie Hancock, also turned to funk and other black musical styles, incorporating them and occasionally 'gimmicks' into their performances. Performers include:

Herbie Hancock **Joe Zawinul**
Keith Jarrett **McCoy Tyner**
Chick Corea **Miles Davis**
Wayne Shorter

Revision Questions

1. Name three styles of solo jazz piano playing and a performer of each style.
2. Name three differences between Dixieland and New Orleans jazz.
3. Name two black and two white performers associated with Chicago jazz.
4. Name three characteristics of swing.
5. Name three big band leaders and the instruments they played.
6. What style of jazz flourished in the 1940s? Name two performers who played jazz in this style.
7. What is trad jazz?
8. Name three musical elements of bebop.
9. What is third stream jazz?
10. What is the mixture of jazz and rock called?

(For answers, see page 128.)

Worksheet 2

Listen to examples of the styles listed in the left column and fill in the information needed in the other columns.

Style	Example	Performer	Date	Musical observations
ragtime				
New Orleans				
Dixieland				
Chicago				
swing				

Style	Example	Performer	Date	Musical observations
blues				
boogie-woogie				
bebop				
cool				
free jazz				
third stream				
Latin American				
modern/ electric				
fusion				

Musical Elements in Jazz

1. HARMONY

12 bar blues

The most important harmonic factor of jazz is the use of the 12 bar blues. This is the chord sequence which accompanied the original three-lined songs of the Negro slaves, and uses only three chords in the following pattern*:

This chord sequence became the basis of much early jazz and has remained the backbone of jazz ever since. It is used for improvisation and in composed jazz, and also spread from jazz into many other areas of popular music, such as rock 'n' roll, zydeco, and honky tonk.

Added chords

One of the things which developed in jazz, through improvisation rather than through design, is the use of added chords. An **added chord** is a triad with extra notes not in the triad added on top, that is,

The 'G' refers to the triad, the '7' refers to the note 7 above (=F) which has been added.

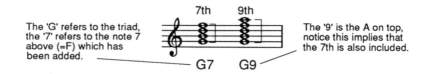

The '9' is the A on top, notice this implies that the 7th is also included.

It is this type of chord which gives jazz its distinctive sound. Try playing the 12 bar blues above using added chords instead of plain triads and notice how the sound and feel of the music are altered.

Substitution

If we played the same chord sequence over and over as the accompaniment to a song or as the basis for a soloist to improvise on, it would become boring. One of the ways of avoiding this is through the use of **chord substitution**. Chord substitution is when a chord is replaced by another one that also fits the harmony. On a simple level this can be done using the triads based on the notes of a scale. Here is a 12 bar blues sequence with a melody on top and underneath a new chord sequence with substitutions; notice that the new chords also fit the melody notes.

*Though it can vary depending on the performer, eg bar 10 often has chord V again and some performers use chord IV in bar 2

One of the most common substitutions is the **tritone substitution**. Here a chord is replaced by the one that is a tritone, or augmented fourth, away. At first this will seem impossible as the original chords, for example,

do not have any common tones to justify the substitution. But if we make each one into an added chord,

the substitution can be easily seen to work.

To see this you need to understand **enharmonics** — this is when a note has more than one way of being written. In the above chords, B♮ and C♭ are the same note, that is, they are enharmonically equal. To make this substitution you are relying on the B♮/C♭ being the same, and F being in both chords, for example,

In a tritone substitution the third of the original chord (B♮ here) becomes the seventh of the substituted one (C♭), and the seventh of the original (F) becomes the third in the new one (F).

Another form of substitution is **melodic substitution**. To do this you take an already composed jazz song, remove the existing melody, keep the chords and write your own melody, or better still improvise one, above them. Try this with a well-known song, for example 'When the Saints Go Marching In', to get the idea and then branch out into more chromatic and complex territory.

The circle of fifths

Like the 12 bar blues, this is a chord sequence that has been used as the basis of composition and improvisation. It is found in many other types of music as well as jazz, and has been a recognised harmonic device for centuries. It was, for instance, common in the 18th century in music by Vivaldi and Mozart.

The circle of fifths simply means that the starting chord is treated as the fifth triad (dominant) of the next chord. This results in the following pattern,

which, if it is too long, can be shortened by making one of the steps a tritone instead of a fifth.

The second section (bars 15 to 20) of *Take Five* by Paul Desmond uses this chord pattern.

TAKE FIVE

Moderately Fast

Music by Paul Desmond
Lyrics by Lola and Dave Brubeck

Chord symbols

The range of chords used in jazz is extensive. Because jazz should correctly not be written down, players perform from chord charts which use a set of accepted chord symbols. The following are the main ones you will need to read, they will also show you how to interpret any others you may come across.

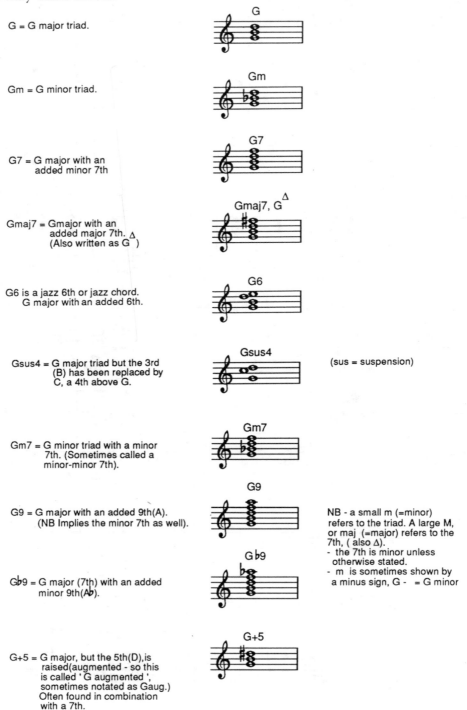

G = G major triad.

Gm = G minor triad.

G7 = G major with an added minor 7th

Gmaj7 = Gmajor with an added major 7th. Δ
(Also written as G^Δ)

G6 is a jazz 6th or jazz chord. G major with an added 6th.

Gsus4 = G major triad but the 3rd (B) has been replaced by C, a 4th above G.

(sus = suspension)

Gm7 = G minor triad with a minor 7th. (Sometimes called a minor-minor 7th).

G9 = G major with an added 9th(A). (NB Implies the minor 7th as well).

Gb9 = G major (7th) with an added minor 9th(Ab).

NB - a small m (=minor) refers to the triad. A large M, or maj (=major) refers to the 7th, (also Δ).
- the 7th is minor unless otherwise stated.
- m is sometimes shown by a minus sign, G - = G minor

G+5 = G major, but the 5th(D),is raised(augmented - so this is called ' G augmented ', sometimes notated as Gaug.) Often found in combination with a 7th.

34

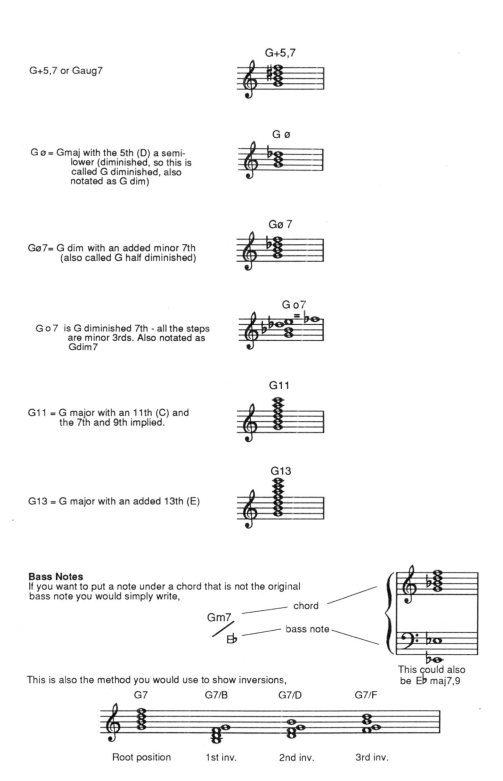

G+5,7 or Gaug7

G ⌀ = Gmaj with the 5th (D) a semi-
lower (diminished, so this is
called G diminished, also
notated as G dim)

G⌀7= G dim with an added minor 7th
(also called G half diminished)

G o 7 is G diminished 7th - all the steps
are minor 3rds. Also notated as
Gdim7

G11 = G major with an 11th (C) and
the 7th and 9th implied.

G13 = G major with an added 13th (E)

Bass Notes
If you want to put a note under a chord that is not the original
bass note you would simply write,

Gm7

chord

bass note

This could also
be E♭ maj7,9

This is also the method you would use to show inversions,

G7   G7/B   G7/D   G7/F

Root position   1st inv.   2nd inv.   3rd inv.

Knowing how to read the chord symbols of a chart is only the beginning of interpreting
them and turning them into a piece of music. While for instance the symbol G△ means to play
a G major chord with an added major seventh, it does not mean that a keyboard player would

35

play this,

with both hands, as this would be too heavy a sound. It is more usual to play something like this,

The way the notes of the chord are distributed when played is called **voicing** and the example above shows a good rule to remember when trying to work out how to interpret a chord symbol. Keep the widest gap in the chord in the bass and the closer gaps in the upper part. You will need to know how to work out **inversions** of chords to achieve the best sound in the right hand parts, for example,

Notice also that there is no need to include every note of the original chord. The notes that are necessary are the bass, the third of the chord, and the added notes (the ones shown by the numbers next to the chord). So G△ is acceptable as

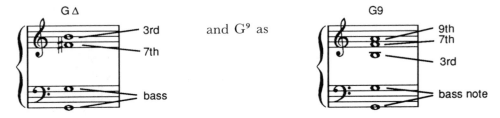

and G⁹ as

Another important aspect of voicing is being able to connect the chords so they have their own musical identity and establish some sort of musical flow. To interpret the chord sequence C7 F7 B♭m7 E♭7 as

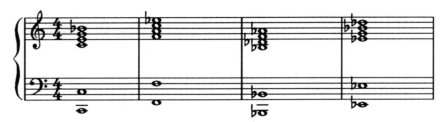

would sound very disjointed and bumpy. A better version would be

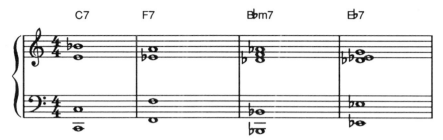

While the bass moves up and down by leaps, the right hand part has been voiced so a line like a melody results. Notice how unessential notes have been left out of the interpretation of the symbols.

Usually the rhythm of the chords is notated in some form of shorthand, either with **vergules** (like in rock guitar music),

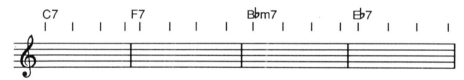

or with the tails of notes.

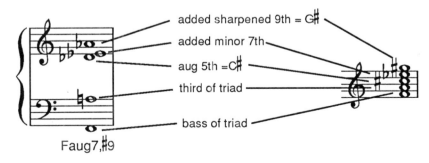

Sometimes the rhythm is left entirely up to the players and their feel for fitting in with the other instruments and the style of the music.

Chromatic development

As jazz went through its historical periods, one of the things that changed was its range of chromatic harmony. Chromatic harmony uses notes that don't correctly belong to the key of a piece. While New Orleans jazz can be played without any chord additions beyond the seventh, by the time of bebop, chromaticism in jazz had reached a very advanced stage. This has remained with jazz so it is not unusual to find chord symbols such as, $F_{aug}^{7,\#9}$. While these may look daunting, their interpretation follows the same rules that apply for the simple symbols, that is,

added sharpened 9th = G♯

added minor 7th

aug 5th = C♯

third of triad

bass of triad

Faug7,♯9

NOTE: In the interpretation the accidentals have all been enharmonically changed for ease of reading.

but because of the possible dissonances the voicings are very important. In these examples the possibility of playing A natural and A flat next to each other has been alleviated by removing them to the distance of a ninth. Notice how the chord has been spaced to leave gaps and allow the potential dissonances to create their effect.

If we applied a tritone substitution to this chord we would have,

Faug7,♯9/B

2. RHYTHM

Rhythm is probably the most important element of jazz and what most people would mean when they talk of a piece of music sounding 'jazzy'. It is also the hardest element to pin down and notate because of the improvisatory nature of jazz. There are, however, three musical factors which help create the rhythmic effect of jazz — syncopation, anticipation, and cross rhythm.

Syncopation occurs when the normal accent is displaced, when it is put on any other beat or note than the first and third in a bar of $\frac{4}{4}$. At its simplest, syncopation happens in the backbeat pattern common in snare drum parts, $\left(\frac{4}{4} \; \prime \; \downarrow \; \prime \; \downarrow \right)$, where the accent is on the second and fourth beats in the bar. Ragtime (see page 1) relies for its musical identity on a highly syncopated melodic line against the march like rhythms of the left hand part,

38

Anticipation is the name given to when a note is sounded just before it should sound. If we take the first phrase of 'When the Saints Go Marching In',

and introduce some anticipation, we would have,

Cross rhythm is the contrast set up between two rhythms being played at the same time. The effect of syncopation and regular beat in ragtime is an example of this.

Different jazz rhythms

Though rhythm is hard to notate in improvised solo melodic playing, there are standard rhythms, usually played by the rhythm section, for the different styles of jazz. This is one way we can identify the different types of jazz, as the rhythms are quite distinct.

New Orleans and **Chicago** jazz favour a steady $\frac{4}{4}$ feel with bass drum on the accented beats and a backbeat on the snare,

Piano parts in this style often use a vamp or stride style of playing which also strengthens this rhythm,

In **Swing**, $\frac{4}{4}$ is relaxed to a $\frac{12}{8}$ feel by lengthening the first quaver of each pair, becoming in $\frac{4}{4}$ or in $\frac{12}{8}$. Players of melodic parts must remember to also do this as their music is usually written straight ( ) but with the instruction 'swing feel' or the indication . A typical swing drumkit rhythm would be,

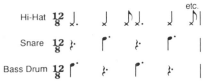

Bebop, being a reaction to New Orleans, Chicago, and swing, had new ideas about rhythm. In general the speed of bebop is faster and, because an important part of its melodic improvisation is arpeggiation of the underlying chords or the use of scalic passages created by introducing passing notes into these arpeggios, the rhythmic drive of bebop, in the upper parts, comes from a continual stream of quavers. Don't forget though that these will be phrased and accented to create syncopation so the music does not sound as if it is in a steady $\frac{4}{4}$, for instance,

The underlying drum rhythms of bebop can be very complicated, but we can identify some characteristics which help create the style. First, the ride cymbal plays all the time, usually repeated quavers (this is also responsible for the timbral texture of bebop). The snare drum is used to throw in off beat accents — very short and sharp — that are referred to as 'shots'. The bass drum avoids the first beat of the bar, thus removing any sense of a firm rhythmic starting point, and drops in with syncopated rhythms or individual notes called 'explosions'. Polyrhythm can often be the result of all these things, and this adds to the rhythmic ambiguity of the style.

Sometimes in bebop there is what is called 'African style' in which the floor tom-tom takes over the repeated quavers of the ride cymbal. A bebop rhythm set up could look like this,

Ride Cymbal

Snare

Bass Drum

After bebop, **cool** returns to a more definite rhythmic feel though again different. Now although the bass drum repossesses the first beat of the bar, its rhythms become dotted,

Repeated notes on the ride cymbal are out and a subtler use of the hi-hat takes over, not being used all the time but to accentuate certain rhythms. Cool also sees the introduction of new styles of rhythmic interest influenced by Latin American music. Often in cool you will find the clave rhythm, played as a rim shot on the snare drum, and the rhythms of the samba, cha-cha, or bossa nova mixed into the overall rhythmic web. At the same time groups began using Latin American instruments and percussionists.

Cool also used uneven time signatures, such as $\frac{5}{4}$ and $\frac{7}{4}$. A good example of $\frac{7}{4}$ is Dave Brubeck's *Unsquare Dance* which uses the following rhythmic patterns,

UNSQUARE DANCE

By D. Brubeck

(**NB:** This is a 12 bar blues bass reduced to six bars of $\frac{7}{4}$)

As its name implies **free jazz** is free and anything can happen. Rhythmically this means changing time signatures, shifting accents, intense syncopation, and free rhythmic improvisation.

3. MELODY

The blues scale

There are many versions of the blues scale, and opinions differ as to its origin and use. The difference between the versions concerns the number of notes. The sparsest one is

which is pentatonic. Other versions add more notes,

until the final one which has nine notes,

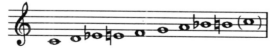

While the flattened third (E flat) and seventh (B flat) are present all the time, there is controversy over the flattened fifth (G flat).

What is even more confusing is that the scales at times don't correspond with the melodic lines supposedly drawn from them. For example, the pentatonic scale is meant to be the basis for blues songs, but if we compare it with a three-lined blues from the late 19th century,

we can see that there are notes in the song that are not in the scale. What are in the song, however, are the **blue notes** — a flattened third in this example — followed sometimes by their 'correct' versions.

While we can agree that the blues scale is important in the melodic construction of jazz, we must always bear in mind that there are no hard and fast rules about it. What is important is the use of blue notes which create chromatic slides and clashes against the accompanying chords, and were the vocal effects that instrumentalists tried to imitate by slides on trombones, playing semitone crush notes on pianos, and falling off notes on trumpets and clarinets. It is these effects which give jazz, especially early jazz, its specific melodic style.

If we compare the second version of the blues scale (on page 41) that includes E flat and B flat,

with the Dorian mode starting on C, we can see that they are the same.

For this reason it is quite correct to say that much jazz is modal, and in the 1950s this became a particular style of jazz, found for example in the works of John Coltrane. In modal jazz it is usual for both the chords and melody to come from the one mode, unlike blues-based jazz in which there is the discrepancy between a blues scale melody and the 12 bar blues chords.

4. FORMAL STRUCTURE

While jazz can and does use many different musical forms, there are two which are very important and which are associated with two separate periods of jazz history. These are the one based on the 12 bar blues, and the 32 bar song form.

12 bar blues

Many early jazz pieces, especially in New Orleans and Chicago style, are based on a number of repetitions of the 12 bar chord sequence. Usually within the group of players each of the melodic instruments has its own **break** in which it plays its improvisation on the melody being used. Sometimes the rhythm instruments, piano, bass, and drums, also have a break. As most pieces start and finish with all the instruments playing, a plan for a piece of New Orleans jazz could look like this:

Tutti — cornet break — clarinet break — trombone break — rhythm break — tutti.

32 bar song form

This plan, still popular, was common during the 1930s and 1940s and belongs to the period of swing jazz. The 32 bars are divided into four lots of eight bars each,

bars 1 – 8, 9 – 16, 17 – 24, 25 – 32
     A   A   B   A   ,

As the letters under the bar numbers show, this is a ternary form in which the first A is immediately repeated. The A sections in such a jazz song are called the **head**, and the B section, the **bridge**.

'Skylark' (1942), words by Johnny Mercer, and music by Hoagy Carmichael, is an example of a 32 bar song form. Play and sing it through, noticing the complicated harmonies and the use of the blue notes in the melody (the notes are circled).

SKYLARK

Music by Hoagy Carmichael
Lyrics by Johnny Mercer

43

love can be?_____ Is there a mea-dow in the mist,_____ Where some-one's

wait-ing to be kissed SKY_____ LARK,_____ Have you seen a val - ley

green with Spring,_____ Where my heart can go a jour-ney - ing_____

O-ver the sha-dows and the rain, to a blos-som cov-ered lane?___ And in your

lone-ly flight,_____ Have-n't you heard the mu-sic in the night_____

Won-der-ful mu-sic, Faint as a "will o' the wisp," Cra - zy as a loon

Sad as a gyp - sy ser - e - nad - ing the moon.__ (Oh,)

SKY - LARK,_____ I don't know if you can find these things,_____

__ But my heart is rid - ing on your wings,_____ So, if you see them an - y

where, Won't you lead me there?_____ there?_____

Dal Segno
al Fine

Fine

5. BASS LINES

The bass player, whether using a tuba, trombone, double bass, or electric bass, is very important in jazz. He or she works with the keyboard player and drummer to create the rhythmic background for the other instruments and also needs to know how to make up interesting bass lines. The simplest thing a bassist can do is to fill in the gaps between the bass notes of chords in a pattern, for example in a 12 bar blues,

If we take this one step further and have the same type of movement in all the bars, the bass line will start to sound interesting and give character to the music.

To do this there are a number of standard patterns the bassist can use,

47

Notice that these use the flattened seventh of the blues scale (B flat in these examples) and use semitones to arrive at the right note at the next bar (example 4). If we combine these patterns under a 12 bar sequence we would have this,

which is the beginning of a characteristic jazz bass line. Once you know the patterns, like anything else, you have to use them and experiment with your own ideas and developments.

6. IMPROVISATION

Improvisation is the core of jazz, and is something which can only really be learnt through practical work and listening to other players. Here, however, are some ideas to help you get started on improvisation. First you need to know that there are different types of jazz improvisation depending on the musical basis you are using. Three types are **blues**, **substitution**, and **modal**.

Blues improvisation implies that the harmony will be a 12 bar blues and the melodic part will use a blues scale with the all important blue notes. Substitution will require reading from the chord chart of an already composed song and replacing the melody with one of your own. Modal improvisation means that a mode will be used for both the chords and the melodic line. The two best modes to use are the Aeolian,

and the Dorian,

because they both have a minor sound typical of blues, and show similarities to blues scales.

For our purposes there are two main processes of improvisation — improvisation around an existing melody, and improvisation of new melodic material.

Improvisation around an existing melody

To work around an existing melody there are a number of simple devices you can use which when added together will result in quite complex results. First, remember to alter the rhythm by syncopating or anticipating notes, or you could 'swing' the rhythm by replacing

♫ with ♩ ♪. At various times in jazz history (1920s for example) dotted rhythms were

popular instead of ♩♩ , try this as well.

When it comes to changing the actual melody, if they are not there, add blue notes. Remember also that melodies can be altered by the use of passing notes that fill in gaps. If there are two people playing you can try question and answer techniques, as in these three examples of the same opening phrase from 'When the Saints Go Marching In'.

1. Uses only one note for the answer

2. Imitates the original notes

3. Answers with something different

Adding an independent polyphonic part to an existing piece is part of the sound we recognise in New Orleans jazz — usually this sort of part is played by the trombone, or in the upper register by the clarinet. To do this you can use the new melody written as melodic substitution at the same time as the existing melody is played. This will give you some ideas on how this type of early jazz collective improvisation works.

Improvising new melodic material

To do this you need to be able to read the chord chart that the other players will be using for accompaniment, or have very good listening powers to pick up the changes in harmony as they occur.

For melody line instruments, remember that your part does not have to have lots of notes and that sometimes the most successful improvisations are limited in their range. Simpler is often better, so start by looking for the notes that are common to chords in a series, called **common tones**, and centre your work around them. Once you feel confident with this approach try arpeggiation of the chords on the chart,

and then using passing notes to create scale-like passages. Remember to use rhythmic variations and create phrases with shape, not just any stream of notes.

Keyboard players have to be able to perform two separate roles when improvising from a chord chart — accompanying, called **comping**, as part of the rhythm section, and improvising solo sections, called **breaks**.

Comping is a very important part of the keyboard player's technique: the player has to provide both a rhythmic feel and the harmony for the soloist to play from. At the same time the keyboard must not overshadow the solo line, so you must listen closely and use your musical judgement as you play to know when to lighten the sound. At the same time the keyboard player has the responsibility to work in with the solo instrument, complementing its line with musical interplay including question and answer techniques, and fills when the soloists stops for a breath or phrase break.

Like the melodic line instruments, keyboard players should start with simple techniques for their solo breaks. Try using the notes of the chord, for example,

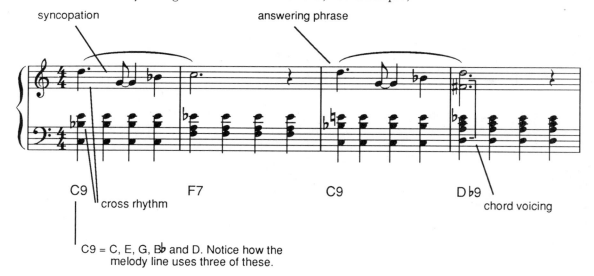

C9 = C, E, G, B♭ and D. Notice how the melody line uses three of these.

Notice how this example has many jazz characteristics — it has syncopation, answering phrases, cross rhythm, and shows voicing of the chords — yet it only uses the notes of the chord as indicated by the chord symbols.

Bass players will also need to improvise when playing from a chart as they do not simply play the bottom note of each chord but have to fill in the missing notes and create interest. As jazz progresses through its style developments, the bass parts alter, becoming more complex and funky, that is more rhythmically interesting. Here are some representative bass patterns for some of the different jazz styles; they all use the same chords as the piano part above.

Some points to remember when improvising

- decide on the musical basis — blues, substitution, modal
- decide on creating new material or working around an existing piece
- start with simple devices, common tones and arpeggios
- add passing notes to arpeggios
- think of using question and answer techniques
- remember to use rhythmic variations
- listen to the other players and play with them not against them
- remember what sounds good and works and try to use it again

Improvisation activity

Here is the music for 'When the Saints Go Marching In'. Use it for the basis of class improvisations by:
(a) improvising around the melody
(b) adding answering phrases to the melody on a second instrument
(c) doing chord substitution on the chords
(d) doing melodic substitution by making up a new melody to fit the chords
(e) playing the original melody and the new one together
(f) adding an independent bass line
(g) using the chord chart as the basis for group improvisation.

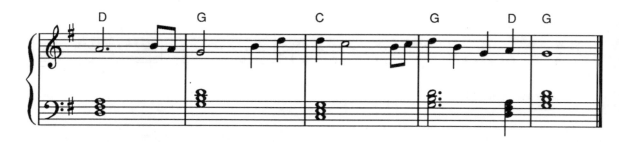

Vocabulary revision

Define each of the following jazz terms.*

12 bar blues	stride piano playing
added chord	swing rhythm
substitution	clave rhythm
circle of fifths	blues scales
tritone substitution	blue note
chord chart	modal jazz
inversion	32 bar song form
vergule	head
voicing	bridge
syncopation	improvising
anticipation	common tone
cross rhythm	comping
vamping	break

*Answers can be checked from the Glossary, page 133.

Worksheet 3

Choose some examples of different styles of jazz and for each one fill in this worksheet by writing a comment for each element.

Title of music	
Writer	
Performer	Date
Musical element	**Comment**
Rhythm	
Harmony	
Formal structure	
Melody/scale form	
Style of jazz	

Instruments in Jazz

Jazz can be performed by any combination of instruments, from an unaccompanied solo, small groups or combos, to big bands (with between 20 and 30 players). The usual jazz combinations attempt to create a balance of firstly, tone colours (or timbres) between instruments and secondly, roles — rhythmic, melodic and harmonic.

THE RHYTHM SECTION

Jazz is commonly written in $\frac{4}{4}$ time but played with a 'swing' feel. The various rhythmic intricacies which cause the music to 'swing' include syncopation (emphasising the weak beats or misplacing the accents), cross meters and polyrhythms.

The rhythm section is the backbone of the jazz group. Its role is to maintain the steady, underlying pulse, leaving the melody instruments to exploit the offbeats and syncopations. In practice, however, the rhythm section often plays a harmonic role as well as a rhythmic one. The rhythm section usually includes drums, a bass instrument like a double (or string) bass, electric bass guitar or tuba, and often a piano (the rhythmic role being supplied principally by the left hand).

Drums

The role of the drums in Afro-American music and jazz can be traced back to their African roots. Drums are synonymous with music in Africa. They are used to accompany all aspects of the African lifestyle — singing, dancing, important ceremonies and celebrations. The natural sense of rhythm the Africans possessed and the important role that music played in their lives was carried with them when they were taken as slaves to the New World.

Many white slave owners in America tried to ban the use of drums among the slaves as they were afraid drums would be used to incite revolt. (In some African regions 'talking' drums are still used today to convey messages over vast distances.) In spite of the ban drumming could still be heard publicly in some parts of the South, for example on Sundays in Congo Square, the French controlled area of New Orleans. Body percussion and singing couldn't be eliminated and singing and vocalising became the primary 'instrument' of the developing black American music.

After the War of Independence (1775–1783) drums became more widespread as an outcome of the presence of military bands. The drums played an important role in the street bands of New Orleans in the late 19th and early 20th centuries. These marching bands, playing as they did for parades and funerals were a forerunner of the 20th century jazz bands, and the role and importance of the drums in maintaining a steady beat was established.

The first drumkits were simple — bass drum, snare and ride cymbal (sometimes with other percussion instruments such as cow bells). Throughout the following decades, drumkits increased in size with the addition of toms and other cymbals. Their role was to maintain a solid $\frac{4}{4}$ rhythmic foundation. During the bebop era of the 1940s the role of the drummer developed in importance. Instead of merely maintaining the straight beat with the emphasis on bass drum, the drummer began to play the pulse on cymbal producing a light, sparkling tone quality to back the ensemble while the bass drum was kept for special effects. This left one hand free to create exciting and different counter rhythms to the other performers. The role of the drums has maintained its importance ever since. Some famous drummers include:

Paul Barbarin (Louis Armstrong, Luis Russell)
Art Blakey (Jazz Messengers, Thelonius Monk, Horace Silver)
Cozy Cole
Baby (Warren) Dodds (Louis Armstrong)
Lionel Hampton

The Campbelltown Camden District Marching Band

Art Blakey

Gene Krupa (Benny Goodman)
Buddy Rich (Charlie Parker)
Max Roach (Clifford Brown, Charlie Parker, Sonny Rollins)

Activity

Draw and label the parts of the drumkit.

Listening

Listen to some examples of jazz. Can you hear the drummer? Complete the following table.

Example	Performers and drummer (if known)	Era	Role of the drummer (pulse, effects, cross rhythms etc)

Keyboards

The piano has always been a central instrument in the development of jazz. Its importance rests on its ability to incorporate the roles of rhythm, harmony and melody. The piano's role in jazz is as both a soloist as well as part of ensembles.

Ragtime, popular in the last quarter of the 19th century, was a notated style for solo piano. The left hand maintained a steady beat, usually in 'oom-pah' or stride style, that is, with a low left hand note played on the first and third beats, followed by chords on beats 2 and 4. The right hand played the syncopated melody. Though written for solo instrument, ragtime's form was derived from the march, where a number of contrasting sections are linked together to form a whole.

In the early Dixieland groups the piano provided the beat as well as giving the harmonies underneath the improvised melodies of trumpet and clarinet.

Women first played a role as performer and composer during the Dixieland period. The piano was one of the few instruments accepted as a performing medium for women in early jazz groups. Pianists from this era include Lil Hardin (Louis Armstrong's wife and pianist in King Oliver's Creole Jazz Band and Louis Armstrong's Hot Five (1920s)), Marge Creath (St Louis Band), and later Mary Lou Williams (in the 1930s) and Maryanne McPartland. The tradition continues today with Blossom Dearie and Australia's Judy Bailey.

Boogie-woogie was a style of piano playing that came from Chicago and Kansas City. It was a fast version of the 12 bar blues with a steady and characteristic left hand style. Pianists famous for this manner of playing include:

Albert Ammons   **Jimmy Yancy**
Meade 'Lux' Lewis   **Clarence 'Pinetops' Smith**
Pete Johnson

eg 1. 'Boogie Woogie'

eg 2. 'Barrelhouse'

Try and put a syncopated treble (right hand) above the chord progressions given. The simplest right hand part would be to play merely the chords on the first and fourth or second and fourth beats.

Stride playing was a development of ragtime and was characterised by wide leaps in the left hand. It was a forerunner of swing and was popular around the 1930s. Some performers include:

James P Johnson   **Art Tatum**
Willie 'The Lion' Smith   **Errol Garner (1940s)**
Fats Waller

The big band era of the 1930s often had pianists as their arrangers and leaders. Because of the numbers of performers involved, improvisation by the whole group was difficult. Parts had to be written for everyone to play and pianists often had the musical skills to do this. Some pianists/arrangers of the period include Count Basie, Duke Ellington, Earl (Fatha) Hines, Fletcher Henderson and Stan Kenton.

The smaller groups of the 1940s (bebop), 1950s and the early 1960s allowed the harmonic potential of the piano to develop. Chords (harmonies) became much more dissonant and the playing style changed. The driving pulse of the 1930s and earlier was altered by more complex though subtler syncopations. The piano's role was sparse though significant. Performers you might listen to from this period include:

Dave Brubeck	**Thelonius Monk**
Nat King Cole	**Oscar Peterson**
Bill Evans	**Bud Powell**
Charles Mingus	**Horace Silver**

Dave Brubeck

Many popular songs have become jazz standards. This is often because their chord structure allows for more complex and imaginative arrangements in the jazz idiom.

'Someday My Prince Will Come' is from the 1950s Walt Disney movie *Sleeping Beauty*. It is given here as a solo piano arrangement.

SOMEDAY MY PRINCE WILL COME

By Churchill and Morey

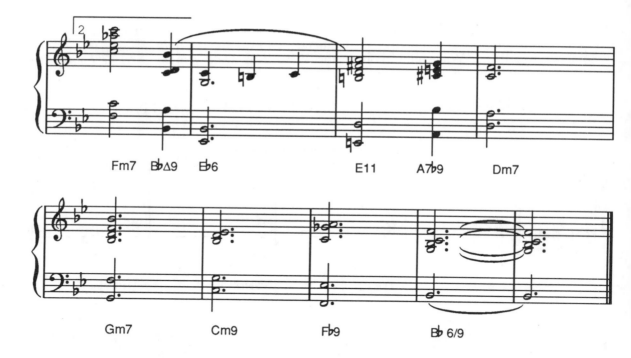

Fm7 Bb△9 Eb6   E11 A7b9 Dm7

Gm7   Cm9   Fb9   Bb 6/9

Questions

1. What is the time signature? Write it in on the music. This time signature means it is in ____ time.
2. What key is the piece written in? (**Hint**: look at the first and last chords.)
3. Write out the key signature here and its scale.

4. This arrangement makes use of additive chords.

   What does this mean?

   What does this do to the sound?

5. What is a 'cycle of fifths'?

   Circle the cycle of fifths in the arrangement.

6. What do the notations G7⁺ and Eb⁰ mean?

7. Would you describe this arrangement as chromatic or diatonic? Why?

8. What do the signs ⌐1⌐ ⌐2⌐ mean?

9. Considering this was a simple song, how has it been turned into a piece of jazz?

(For answers, see page 129.)

60

The piano has remained an important instrument in jazz since the 1950s, though styles have continued to change. Modal influences (pioneered by Bill Evans) have influenced many pianists. The electric keyboard became popular in the 1970s with performers such as **Chic Corea, Herbie Hancock**, and **Keith Jarrett**. The New Wave sounds of the 1970s (Corea and Jarrett)incorporated acoustic and electric keyboards. Fusion, a mixture of jazz and rock also had its pianists like **Joe Zawinal** and **McCoy Tyner**.

McCoy Tyner

Listening

1. Listen to a piece of ragtime. Can you work out the form of the piece? (**Hint:** use a different letter name for each new section.)
2. Listen to a march (eg by Sousa, a famous American march composer). Are there any similarities in the form between the march and ragtime?
3. Listen to and note the similarities and differences between all three solo piano styles, that is, ragtime, boogie-woogie and stride.
4. Complete this table from your listening.

Performer	Era	Name of piece	Style of playing

Bass

Bass instruments that can be included in the rhythm section include double or string bass, electric bass, and tuba (sometimes saxophone). Their role is harmonic, providing the bass line, as well as rhythmic.

The tuba was adapted from its use in the marching bands of New Orleans to become the primary bass instrument in Dixieland. It maintains a steady beat while supplying the harmonic bass.

The double bass or string bass appeared in the small combos that performed around New Orleans. Depending on the instruments available string bass and tuba were interchangeable. The double bass gradually took over the role of primary bass instrument in the rhythm section. It was usually plucked making it more percussive in its attack. The double bass can be heard in all styles of jazz from Chicago (a development of New Orleans jazz), throughout the big band era of the 1930s, in the small combos of bebop in the 1940s, in 1950s cool, and in the free jazz of the 1960s.

The electronic sounds of the mid-1960s and later led to the introduction of the electric bass. The bass guitar's strings are tuned the same as the acoustic bass giving us an indication of its origins. The invention of the fretless bass (primarily for playing fusion) was an attempt to gain the sound and capabilities of the acoustic bass, such as sliding between notes, combined with the dynamic range and sustain of the amplified electric bass.

Famous bass players include:

Charles Mingus
Ray Brown (Modern Jazz Quartet)

Scott LaFaro (Bill Evans)
Eddie Safranski (swing)

Guitar and banjo

The guitar was actually on the scene before jazz as we know it began. The early black Americans created simple home-made string instruments to accompany their singing. A guitar-like instrument made a perfect complement to the voice as it could imitate the slides, bends and dips of the developing black singing style, the blues. Its plaintive sound could interpret the blues second only to the voice. The guitar could play the blues solo or accompany the voice.

The banjo became part of the rhythm section during the Dixieland era. Gradually in Chicago style jazz (late 1920s) the guitar superseded the banjo, perhaps because of its more sophisticated 'city' sound compared to the country sounds of the banjo with its connotations of black and white minstrel shows. The guitar itself dropped out of favour at the end of the big band era as jazz groups whittled down their sound to piano, bass, drums, trumpet and saxophone. String instruments, especially the guitar remained popular jazz instruments in Europe and eventually the guitar returned to jazz in the 1970s in an amplified form with jazz rock fusion. The electric guitar is now a standard part of the rhythm section of jazz, especially in stage bands and West Coast commercial jazz (1970s to 1980s).

Guitarists include:

Big Bill Broonzy
Eddie Condon
Charlie Christian
Django Rheinhardt
Barney Kessel
Eddie Lang

Leadbelly (Huddie Ledbetter)
Johnny St Cyr (banjo)
Muddy Waters
Michel Legrand
Al Di Meola
Stanley Clark

Research

1. Find out what era these guitarists played in and their style.
2. What do you think are the reasons for the decline in popularity of guitars in jazz during the 1940s, and their absence for the next 20 years?

Muddy Waters

BRASS (HORNS)

Brass instruments are conical lengths of tubing wound around for convenience of handling. The player buzzes against the mouthpiece at the narrow end making the air inside the tube vibrate. Valves (or a slide) allow the player to alter the length of the tube, changing the pitch of the note, and a bell at the end of the instrument projects the sound outwards. Other changes to the sound can be made by the way the player blows into the instrument, the different fingerings on the valves and the use of mutes. Any suitable tube, including animal horns and shells, can produce a sound in this way.

At the end of the American Civil War in 1865, many blacks began playing the brass instruments (bugles and cornets) left over from the warring factions. Marching bands and brass bands were also common forms of musical entertainment in the 1800s and so the use of brass instruments in the earliest jazz groups is understandable. Many of the earliest Dixieland standards are in fact marches, and on the streets of New Orleans today street bands play Dixieland jazz as they walk around. *St Louis Blues* and *St James Infirmary* are two standard jazz march tunes particularly associated with Dixieland.

Trumpet and cornet

The trumpet and cornet have been perhaps the most favoured instruments throughout jazz history. They are similar in size (the cornet is a little chunkier and easier to play) and play the same range. Their timbre is bright and brassy.

The trumpet can be played with brilliance and it can also be played sensitively and expressively. Like the guitar, it can imitate the slides and intonations of the human voice — perhaps another reason for its use by the early black jazz musicians — as well as produce unusual sound effects.

The flugelhorn, larger than the trumpet and producing a richer tone, is also a popular instrument in jazz. Famous trumpeters include:

Louis (Satchmo) Armstrong
Buck Clayton (Count Basie, Billie Holiday, Lester Young)
Bill Coleman (Luis Russell, Lester Young)
Miles Davis (flugelhorn, trumpet)
Vince Jones (Australian trumpeter/singer)
Maynard Ferguson (Stan Kenton)
Harry James (Benny Goodman)
Bunk Johnson (Sidney Bechet)
Wynton Marsalis
Fats Navarro (Charlie Parker)
Red Nichols (Benny Goodman, Jack Teagarden)
King Oliver
Charlie Shavers (Sidney Bechet, Tommy Dorsey, Charlie Parker)
Joe Smith (Fletcher Henderson, Ma Rainey, Bessie Smith)
Mugsy Spanier (Sidney Bechet, Bix Beiderbecke)
Rex Stewart (Duke Ellington)
Cootie Williams (Duke Ellington, Benny Goodman, Lionel Hampton)
Dizzy Gillespie

Trombone

This was a popular instrument during the big band era owing to its smooth tone and good group sounds. Its versatility meant that it could play melodic lines as well as filling out the texture between the high melodic instruments and bass and it could also produce some distinctive sounds (especially those glissandi well known to Dixieland). It began to be replaced by the tenor sax during the Chicago period (1930s) and, like many other instruments, it became less popular with the development of the small jazz combos of the late 1940s and 1950s.

Performers include:

Bob Brookmeyer (valve trombone — Stan Getz, Clark Terry)
George Brunis (Eddie Condon, New Orleans Rhythm Kings)
Tommy Dorsey
Maynard Ferguson (valve trombone — Stan Kenton)
Bill Harris (Gene Krupa)
J J Johnson (Miles Davis, Stan Getz, Sonny Rollins, Sonny Stitt)
Glenn Miller
Joseph 'Tricky Sam' Nanton (Duke Ellington)
Kid Ory (Louis Armstrong, Johnny Dodds, Jelly Roll Morton)
Jack Teagarden (Louis Armstrong, Benny Goodman)

Glenn Miller

Vince Jones

Louis Armstrong

Listening

What horn (brass) players did you hear? Was there anything distinctive about their playing?

Performer	Era	Name of piece	Instrumentation	Playing style/ features

REEDS

The two most important reed instruments used in jazz are the clarinet and saxophone. Their sound is made when the player sets up vibrations in a reed (a thin piece of bamboo) fitted over a hole in the mouthpiece.

The clarinet and saxophone are relatively new instruments. The clarinet as we know it today was developed during the mid-18th century. Mozart was one of the first composers to write effectively for it. The saxophone was invented in 1846 by a Belgian called Adolphe Sax, in an attempt to blend the sound of the clarinet with that of a brass instrument.

Clarinet

The clarinet is fondly called a 'licorice stick' by Dixieland players. Its unmistakeable sound and its ease in playing rapid, virtuosic scales and runs made it a popular 'front line' instrument. The clarinet's ability to play easily over a wide range and in different registers, together with its piercing tone quality which allows it to be heard over trumpets, trombones and drums, gave Dixieland one of its distinctive sounds.

Clarinet techniques used frequently in jazz include trills, glissandi, flutter tonguing and crushed notes.

The clarinet was used primarily until the end of the big band era when its role was usurped by the saxophone during the bebop years. There was a slight resurgence in its popularity with Buddy de Franco (cool jazz) in the 1950s. Performers include:

Sidney Bechet (Louis Armstrong)
Bix Beiderbecke (Paul Whiteman)
John Dankworth

Woody Herman
Jimmie Noone (Earl Hines, Johnny Dodds,
    Louis Armstrong)

Buddy de Franco (Sidney Bechet, Jelly Roll Morton)
Johnny Dodds (Louis Armstrong, King Oliver)
Benny Goodman
W C Handy

Pee Wee Russell (Bix Beiderbecke, Jack Teagarden)
Artie Shaw
Lester Young
Don Burrows (Australian)

The Don Burrows Quintet

Saxophone

The instrument most identifiable with the jazz sound is the saxophone. Its tone colour blends in with the horn's brass yet it is capable of competing with it in volume. It is perhaps the most expressive instrument in jazz, able to produce strident sounds or convey melodies needing great sensitivity. The most commonly used saxophones in jazz are the alto and tenor, with the baritone and soprano being used almost as frequently.

The saxophone was played in jazz as early as the 1920s but its role was overshadowed by the clarinet which it replaced as a front line instrument in the late 1920s in the style known as Chicago jazz. The saxophone became much more important in the big bands of the 1930s where several saxophones were combined into their own section. The alto, tenor and, to a lesser extent, baritone saxophones came to the forefront of jazz in the bebop era with the emergence of saxophone virtuosos such as Charlie 'Bird' Parker, Lester 'Prez' Young and Dexter Gordon. The improvisational, technical and interpretative skills of these virtuosos on the saxophone spread its popularity throughout America and Europe.

Performers include:

Sidney Bechet (soprano — Louis Armstrong)
Harry Carney (baritone — Duke Ellington, Lionel Hampton, Billie Holiday)
Benny Carter (alto, tenor — Count Basie, Fletcher Henderson)
Ornette Coleman (alto)
John Coltrane (tenor — Miles Davis, Thelonius Monk)
John Dankworth (alto)
Eddie 'Lockjaw' Davis (tenor — Count Basie)
Jimmy Dorsey (alto)
Bud Freeman (tenor — Louis Armstrong, Jack Teagarden, Benny Goodman)
Stan Getz (tenor — Woody Herman)

67

Coleman Hawkins (tenor — Lionel Hampton, Fletcher Henderson)
Johnny Hodges (alto — Duke Ellington, Earl Hines, Billie Holiday)
Gerry Mulligan (Baritone — Miles Davis)
Charlie 'Bird' Parker (alto)
Dexter Gordon
Sonny Rollins (tenor — Miles Davis, Thelonius Monk, Bud Powell)
Sonny Stitt (Dizzie Gillespie)
Lester (Prez) Young (tenor — Count Basie, Nat King Cole, Coleman Hawkins)

Sonny Rollins

Ornette Coleman

Listening

1. Compare the playing styles of at least two jazz saxophone players.

	Player 1	Player 2	Player 3
Name of performer			
Type of saxophone played			
Era			
Name of tune			
Playing style			

2. Listen to some Dixieland jazz. What is the role of the clarinet? Does it use any 'gimmicks' or technical skills? Describe what you hear.

Name of work	Era	Performer (if known) or group	Instrumentation	Role of clarinet

OTHER INSTRUMENTS

Percussion

Vibes (vibraphones) are often heard in jazz. They were first introduced around the 1930s by Red Norvo and Lionel Hampton. Their distinctive sound was most popularly heard in the Modern Jazz Quartet (MJQ) in the 1960s (Milt Jackson on vibes). Australia's best known vibes player is percussionist John Sangster. Other percussion instruments used in jazz include marimba and xylophone. Congas supplement the drums in jazz with a Latin American flavour.

Keyboards

Early jazz occasionally used the harmonium or organ. Synthesisers and electric pianos are popular in modern jazz.

Wind instruments

Flutes were sometimes used in the big bands of the 1930s. With the use of amplification in the 1960s and the search for new sounds, orchestral instruments such as the flute and oboe have been used to create new effects. Don Burrows is a well-known Australian performer on flute. The harmonica is frequently used in jazz, especially in the blues. Even the French horn has made an entrance as a jazz performer.

Stringed instruments

The violin is perhaps the best known orchestral instrument that has made the transition to jazz. Joe Venuti and Stephane Grappelli popularised this sound.

The voice as instrument

Jazz is a style of music that began as a vocal style. The voice is still a popular way of performing jazz. Often in jazz, the instruments attempt to imitate the nuances of the human voice. Sometimes it is the other way round — the voice attempts to imitate the sounds and virtuosity of an instrument.

Scat singing is the technique of singing using nonsense syllables. Scatting is often improvised as a solo or interspersed with the words of a song. Stylists include:

Mose Allison   **Bobby McFerrin**
Louis Armstrong   **Lambert, Hendricks and Ross**

Revision questions

1. Name three instruments found in a jazz rhythm section.
2. During the bebop period in the 1940s, the drummer's role increased in importance. How did this role change?
3. Classify these pianists into the style or era they played in.

   Art Tatum _____   Lil Hardin _____

   Bill Evans _____   Earl Hines _____

   Albert Ammons _____   Joe Zawinal _____

   Herbie Hancock _____   Errol Garner _____

4. Name two march tunes that are associated with Dixieland jazz.
5. What is a flugelhorn? Name two famous 'horn' players.
6. Give two 'reed' instruments found in jazz and a performer on each.
7. What is a 'licorice stick'? What era of jazz is it most associated with?
8. Put these saxophones in order of size and name a performer on each.

   tenor _____

   baritone _____

   alto _____

   soprano _____

9. Name two orchestral instruments that have been successfully used in jazz and a performer on each.
10. What is 'scatting'?

   (For answers, see page 129.)

Worksheet 4

Choose a piece of jazz in any style and complete the worksheet.

Title	
Performer	**Date recorded**
Style	

Instruments used	Role in overall arrangement, devices used etc

The Influence of Jazz on Other Styles of Music

Since the beginning of the 20th century, jazz has been an important musical influence on other styles of composition. This can be seen in two main areas — other popular music, and the music of 'mainstream' composers.

JAZZ ROCK FUSION

The most important popular style heavily influenced by jazz actually uses the word jazz as part of its name — jazz rock, sometimes known as jazz fusion or just fusion. This is a style of rock music dating from the late 1960s and 1970s and is simply what its name says, a mixture of jazz elements and rock.

The jazz elements most prominent in this style are the use of more complex harmonic progressions than rock, the influence of the 12 bar blues, and the use of jazz oriented instruments such as brass and reeds. The rock elements include the use of rock style basslines, often involving ostinato patterns, the lead guitar style of rock in solo breaks, and the presence of rock drumming patterns and driving rhythms instead of more laid back jazz ones.

The most famous group that performed this style was Chicago; others include Fleetwood Mac, John Mayall's Bluesbreakers, and Blood, Sweat and Tears. While these groups are basically rock groups with some jazz influence, there are other performers which are closer to jazz but have the influence of rock. These include the composers Maynard Ferguson and Steve Weist, and the performer George Benson, particularly in songs such as 'On Broadway'.

Maynard Ferguson

72

MAINSTREAM COMPOSERS

The exoticism of jazz appealed to composers of art music early this century and can be seen in the music of Debussy (1862–1918) in *The Golliwogg's Cakewalk*, and Ravel (1875–1937) in his *Sonata for Piano and Violin*. In Debussy this is seen in the imitation of rhythm, in Ravel in the use of blues sounding chord progressions. Another composer to include jazz influence in his music was Stravinsky (1882–1971) who imitated the instrumentation of early jazz groups in his *Ragtime for 11 Instruments*, and wrote a jazz sounding clarinet concerto called *Ebony Concerto* for Woody Herman. Milhaud (1892–1974) was a keen user of jazz influenced devices, especially jazz inspired rhythms, which can be heard in his ballets *The Ox on the Roof* and *The Creation of the World*. Martinù (1890–1959) was a Czech composer who also wrote chamber music with jazz influence, for example, *Jazz Suite* and *Le Jazz*.

A separate group of composers working in Berlin between the world wars was heavily influenced by jazz. This group included the classically trained composer Kurt Weill (1900–1950) who, after writing operas such as *The Rise and Fall of the City of Mahagonny* which includes cabaret style jazz songs, fled Nazi Germany to become a well-known writer of American musicals. Again, while in America, Weill's music was heavily influenced by jazz and other popular music of the time. Here is an example of a song from *The Rise and Fall of the City of Mahagonny*. Notice the use of chords with added notes and the fills that cover the gaps in the singer's part, for example bar 4 and bars 8-9.

DENN WIE MAN SICH BETTET

(From *The Rise and Fall of the City of Mahagonny*)

Music by Kurt Weill
Words by Bertolt Brecht

73

wür - de en-den im Schau-haus o-der an ei-nem noch shlim-mern
Größ - te auf Er-den ist Lie-be" und "an mor-gen denkt man da

Ort.
nicht" Ja so ein Wort, das ist leicht ge-
Ja Lie - be, das ist leicht ge-

sagt, a-ber ich sa-ge euch daraus wird nichts! Das
sagt, doch so lang man täg-lich äl-ter wird, da

könnt ihr nicht na-chen mit mir! Was aus mir noch wird,das wer-den wir
wird nicht nach Lie-be ge-fragt, da muß man sei-ne kurze Zeit be

seh'n - zen!   Ein   Mensch   ist   kein   Tier!

nüt - zen!   Ein   Mensch   ist   kein   Tier!

75

Perhaps the most famous composer to rely on jazz as an influence is Leonard Bernstein (b1918). Listen to *West Side Story* to see how he uses jazz elements.

Another group of composers falls between the jazz groups and serious composers. This group is typified by George Gershwin (1898–1937) who composed jazz for orchestral instruments. Perhaps his best known music is *Rhapsody in Blue* (1924), originally for piano but later orchestrated to become a mini-concerto. Here is an excerpt from the piano version. Can you find examples of syncopation, blue notes, and sections that are meant to sound like improvisation?

RHAPSODY IN BLUE

By George Gershwin

Revision questions

1. What jazz elements do the following composers use in their jazz influenced compositions?

   Debussy   _____

   Ravel   _____

   Stravinsky   _____

   Weill   _____

   Gershwin   _____

   Milhaud   _____

2. How do the three groups represented by Debussy, Weill, and Gershwin differ in their approach to jazz?
3. How does Gershwin make *Rhapsody in Blue* sound like jazz?
4. Which American composer is perhaps the most famous user of jazz influence?

   _____ What famous musical did he write? _____

(For answers, see page 130.)

Worksheet 5

Listen to examples of both jazz rock and jazz influenced mainstream compositions, identify the jazz elements (rhythm, melody, harmony, instrumentation, blues chords, blue notes, etc) and fill in the worksheet below.

Title of music		
Composer/group		**Date**
Jazz element	**Comment**	

The long quena, a traditional instrument of Southern Peru

FOLK

Folk Music

Folk music is one of the most difficult musical terms to define. Most of the definitions that have been used emphasise that it is passed on aurally through the generations, which suggests that it is 'popular' or has been at some stage, and that it is anonymous or at least the composer is unknown to many who know the songs. What most definitions try to imply is that folk music is separate from the tradition of composed art music (symphonies and so on). Its performing media are usually simple (hence the term 'folk guitar') and its presentation is generally straightforward.

Today it does not matter whether the music is old ('Greensleeves') or modern ('Mr Tambourine Man'), or the composer anonymous (usually abbreviated to anon) or known (Bob Dylan), there is always some feeling of shared ownership of the song and a purpose or relevance of the music to 'the people' as a whole.

As folk music (dances and songs) is part of an aural tradition — the words and music being passed on by learning and repetition — words often change over time and the melodies can appear in different forms. Variations can also occur with each performance through the addition of ornamentation and decoration to the melody, by improvisation, and by varying the accompanying instruments and performing media.

Folk songs throughout the centuries have dealt with and accompanied aspects of everyday life. The style of song varies with the activity it is meant to accompany, so lullabies are soft and slow while work songs are strongly rhythmical.

- Work songs — sea shanties and Afro-American work songs — 'Bound for South Australia'
- Children's songs and game songs — often have an educative, socialising or entertaining role — 'Here We Go Round the Mulberry Bush'
- Religious songs — spirituals, 'Kumbaya', 'Amazing Grace'
- Ballads — narrative songs which tell a story — 'Moreton Bay', 'Barbara Allen'
- Morality songs — 'The House of the Rising Sun'
- Protest songs — 'The Answer is Blowing in the Wind'
- Love songs — 'Greensleeves', 'Barbara Allen'
- Dances are also an important aspect of folk music

The sea shanty 'Bound for South Australia' accompanied the hoisting of the sails on the huge masted ships that sailed the seas before the use of steam, hence it is often referred to as a capstan or halyard shanty. It had a function to perform in that it gave the crew a feeling of solidarity and kept them working together as they hoisted the sails or raised anchor.

The song was led by the shantyman whose job it was to improvise verses and set the pace. The chorus was shouted by the sailors or tars (short for jack tars, as they made the ship watertight by the liberal use of tar).

This questions and answer format is known as call and response and can be found in work songs from around the world including Africa and the songs of the American Negro. They were sung unaccompanied but simple chords are provided for you to play.

BOUND FOR SOUTH AUSTRALIA

Sea Shanty (Anon.)

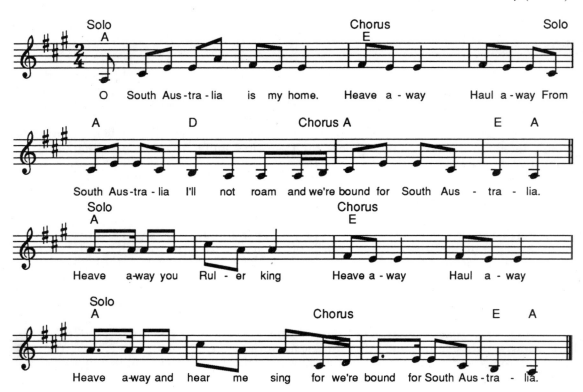

2. And now I'm bound for a distant land
With a bottle of whisky in my hand.

3. I'll drink a glass to a foreign shore
And one to the girl that I adore.

Questions

1. Write another verse in the appropriate style.
2. Mark in the words that the sailors would have sung while pulling at the sail.

HERE WE GO ROUND THE MULBERRY BUSH

Children's Song (Anon.)

Here we go round the mul - berry bush, the mul - berry bush, the mul - berry bush,

Here we go round the mul - berry bush on a cold and fro - sty morn - ing. _____

This is the way we (1) **clean our teeth**

(2) **brush our hair**

(3) **etc.**

European Folk Music

The folk tradition dates back to the Middle Ages. Many itinerant singers and instrumentalists travelled the roads conveying the news, historical information, morality tales and gossip from village to village. These musicians were given the name minstrels or, in France, jongleurs. They accompanied their often long, heroic songs with harps and hurdy-gurdies.

Towards the end of the 11th century another musical class appeared — poet-musicians of often noble birth who sang songs of chivalry, virtuous ladies, love and the partings caused by war. The music was formalised and usually written down as these troubadours or trouvères were well educated. Richard the Lionheart was one of these troubadour kings. The minnesingers (minne = love) were the German equivalent of the troubadours. Their music cannot be said to be folk music (because of their high social class and the fact that we know who wrote much of the music) but their subject matter is similar to that of folk music.

Throughout history folk music continued to play an important unifying role by keeping populations in touch with their cultural and historic roots. Each country and often small regions within each country has its own specific and identifiable folk music with its own style and instrumentation.

Early folk songs were often performed unaccompanied and usually only had one vocal or melodic line.

This little folk song is from Yorkshire in England. It has had a second part added to it (mainly in fourths) giving an 'open', modal or archaic sound to the song. The theme of the song is typical of folksong — an ill-matched marriage. The vocal range is narrow and the song is quite repetitive. Each of the first three bar phrases begins in much the same way. The endings are different and the final phrase hovers around the tonic.

SORRY THE DAY I WAS MARRIED

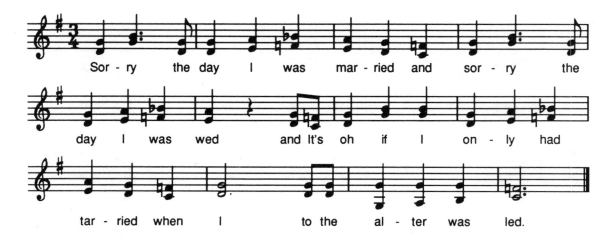

Sor - ry the day I was mar - ried and sor - ry the
day I was wed and It's oh if I on - ly had
tar - ried when I to the al - ter was led.

FOLK MUSIC AND NATIONAL IDENTITY

During the 19th century, people in European countries became increasingly conscious of their national identity. This was partly in response to the political upheavals of the time, as countries shook off the rule of foreign powers or struggled under foreign domination. It was thought that the national spirit could be found in the legends, history and music of the 'common folk', and composers began to use the folk music of their native lands as the inspiration for their melodies. The use of folk-inspired material in the music of composers such as Smetana (Czech, 1824–1884), Liszt (Hungarian, 1811–1886), Tchaikovsky (Russian, 1840–1893), Grieg (Norwegian, 1843–1907), and Sibelius (Finnish, 1865–1957), is often labelled 'nationalism' and it was linked to other attempts in the arts to express the characteristics of a nation through its music, painting, and so on. Good examples of this folk influence can be heard in Tchaikovsky's *Marche Slave*, Liszt's *Hungarian Rhapsodies*, and Grieg's *Norwegian Dances*.

At the same time musicians interested in studying the folk music of different countries began collecting folk songs and dances and notating them. The most famous collectors include Bartók (1881–1945) who worked in Hungary, Bulgaria, Rumania, Turkey and other parts of Asia Minor; Kodály (1882–1967), who collaborated with Bartók; Cecil Sharp (1859–1924) and the Australian Percy Grainger (1882–1961) who both collected music in the British Isles.

Béla Bartók and Zoltán Kodály were famous for their work in collecting and notating the Magyar or traditional music of Hungary. This music, characterised by its modality, specific decoration, irregular rhythms and accents (especially ♪♩) was used in many of their compositions.

Magyar music is not to be confused with the Hungarian 'gypsy' music found in the works of Liszt and Brahms. This music is full of decoration and improvisation. Contrasts of tempo is an obvious feature and there occur abrupt changes of mood and sudden stops.

EIGHTEENTH CENTURY GYPSY MUSIC

(From the movie *Amadeus*)

This music was written at around the same time as Mozart lived and worked. It is featured in the opening court scene of the movie *Amadeus*.

Like many folk dances it begins slowly and gradually increases in tempo (accelerando). Other types of folk music that use accelerandos are the Tora (Jewish), eg *Hava Nagheela*, and Greek folk dancing, eg *Zorba the Greek*. The melody line becomes higher throughout the piece increasing the excitement, while becoming increasingly ornamented and busy in all its parts.

Some of the sections make use of a drone-bass which plays the note G, around which the melody weaves. Drones are common in folk music — the Scots use the bagpipes, the Indian sitar and vina produce drones and the Australian didgeridoo produces a drone. The songs of the troubadours were often accompanied by a vielle, a type of violin which had a drone string. The hurdy-gurdy, a later development of this instrument had several drones.

The tambourine is a typical accompanying instrument. Syncopated at first, it too becomes more frantic in its rhythms as the dance whirls to its conclusion.

Bartók, Kodály, Sharp, and Grainger not only collected folk material but, like other composers of the first half of the 20th century, made arrangements of the music as well. Percy Grainger's arrangements of folk music are particularly well known and include 'Shallow Brown', 'Scotch Strathspey and Reel', 'Lincolnshire Posy', and 'Shepherd's Hey'. Other composers who utilised folk tunes and rhythms in their music include Vaughan Williams (1872–1958, *English Folk Song Suite* and *Fantasia on 'Greensleeves'*), Charles Ives (1874–1954, *Variations on America*), Janáček (1854–1928, *Lachian Dances*), and Aaron Copland (b1900, *Appalachian Spring* and numerous settings of Appalachian songs).

American Folk Music

An important type of early American folk music is the Negro spiritual, a unique blend of Afro and American influences. They are religious songs embodying the experiences and emotions of the early black slaves.

The tempos can be slow and contemplative or rousing and bright. The songs are often in a call and response form, where the response can be identical each time it is heard or varied. Vocal mannerisms include bending, slurring of notes, glides and other decorations.

The themes are basically all similar — a looking forward to a better life where people will be judged by their actions rather than the colour of their skin. Under the guise of moral and religious themes some spirituals told blacks of escape routes to the north and other messages of rebellion.

DIDN'T MY LORD DELIVER DANIEL

85

Spirituals and other black folk music influenced the development of jazz, rhythm and blues, gospel and modern pop music (see page 6).

PROTEST MUSIC

Twentieth century America has also been a fertile ground for the development of folk music. People arrived from many European countries to escape oppression or to find religious and political freedom in a new land and they brought their folk heritage with them. During the Great Depression of the 1930s, many people were homeless and downtrodden and found comfort in the music of Woody Guthrie ('This Land is My Land'), Burl Ives and Leadbelly. Again, in the 1960s America was facing serious social problems including involvement in the Vietnam War, urban decay, racism, and growing youth disillusionment with the American society. The music that seemed to express these feelings most accurately was that of the folk-protest movement. The folk-poet Bob Dylan became its figurehead with such songs as 'Mr Tambourine Man' and 'Hard Rain's a'Gonna Fall'. Others in this movement included Pete Seeger ('Where Have All the Flowers Gone?') and Simon and Garfunkel, whose roots were in the folk tradition.

SIMPLE GIFTS

(SHAKER SONG)

be in the val-ley of love and de-light_____ When true sim-pli-ci-ty is gained To

bow and to bend we shan't be a-shamed To turn, turn will be our de-light 'Till by

turn - ing turn - ing we come round right._____

WOMEN AND THE POPULAR FOLK REVIVAL

Tracy Chapman

    Women have played a significant part in the popular folk revival and the protest movement.
The use of acoustic instruments such as the folk guitar and the lyric quality of many folk songs
allowed women such as Joan Baez, Judy Collins, Joni Mitchell ('Big Yellow Taxi') and Buffy
St Maree ('Universal Soldier') to be at the forefront of the folk-protest movement. Janis Ian
('At Seventeen') and Carol King (*Tapestry* album) wrote many successful songs in the
commercial folk style. There is an ongoing tradition of women singing popular and relevant
folk material today; Tracy Chapman ('Fast Car') and Suzanne Vega ('Small Blue Thing'), are
two current folk singers.

THE QUEEN AND THE SOLDIER

Words and music by Suzanne Vega

$\quad \downarrow = 156$ Bm

The sol - dier came knock - ing up -
"I see you now and you are
How hun - gry are you how

G2   D

on the Queen's door he said "I am not
so ve - ry young but I've seen more battles
weak you must feel as you are living here

A/C♯   D   A

fight - ing for you an - y more" and the
lost than I have bat - tles won and I've
a - lone and you are never re - vealed but I

Bm   G2

Queen knew she'd seen his face some place be -
got this intu - ition says it's all for your
won't march a - gain on your bat - tle

D   A/C♯

fore and slow - ly she let him in - side.
fun and now will you tell me why?"
field and he took her to the win-dow to see.

D   Bm

He said "I've watched your
Well the young Queen she
And the sun it was

G2

pal-ace up here on the hill and I've
fixed him with ar - ro - gant eye said "you
gold through the sky it was grey and

D   A/C#   D

won-dered who's the wo - man for whom we all
won't un - der - stand and you may as well not
she want - ed more than she ev - er could

A   Bm

kill but I am leav - ing to - mor-row and you can
try" but her face was a child's and he
say but she knew how it fright-ened her and

G2   D

do what you will on - ly first I am
thought she would cry but she closed her - self
she turned a - way and would not look at

A/C#   D

ask - ing you why." And she
up like a fan And he said
his face a - gain

G   D/F#

Down the long nar - row hall he was
said "I swal - lowed a secret burn - ing
"I want to live as an hon - est

Esus4

led in - to her room with her
thread it cuts me in - side and
man to get all I de - serve and to

89

ached   and she took him   to   the   door - step   and she

asked   him   to wait   she would   on - ly   be   a

mo-ment   in - side   And

out   in   the   dis - tance   her   or - der   was

heard   and the   sol - dier   was   killed   still

wait-ing   for her   word   and while the   Queen   went on

strang - ling   in the   sol - i - tude   she   pre - ferred   the

bat-tle   con - tin-ued   on.

Music from Other Cultures

All of our examples so far have been from Western music, but it is important to remember that all societies have their own folk music. Here are some examples from Asia and South America. With each one are some comments on its musical style and suggestions on how you might perform it.

LAOS

This is a piece of instrumental music from Laos. Notice the repeated rhythms and the use of a hexatonic scale, . Laotian music, like Korean and Vietnamese, is influenced by Chinese music, especially in the types of instruments used. This piece might typically be played on a two stringed fiddle or bamboo 'mouth organ' with accompaniment on untuned percussion, such as small drum and wood block.

Laotian

VIETNAM

This is a simple strophic song from Vietnam. As with most folk music it repeats a number of melodic ideas. Unlike most folk songs its range is wider than an octave. It uses the pentatonic scale,  so a good idea for some form of accompaniment is to make up

an ostinato from this scale to go with the song. Typical Vietnamese instruments include the moon-lute, dan tranh ('zither'), sona ('oboe'), kovan ('clarinet'), dan nhi ('fiddle'), gongs and drums.

QUA CÂU GIÒ BAY

Yêu_ nhau côi_ 1.noṇ ôi a cho nhau về_
2.yêm
3.nhân

nhà dôi_ rằng cha dôi me_ a, à, a, à, a. Rằng

a ôi a_ qua_ câú rằng a ôi a_ qua

câù Tình tình tình gió_ bay, tình

1&2

3

tình tình gió_ bay._ yêu rôi_

Translation: "The Bridge in the Wind"

1. Because I love you I will give you my hat, (2. cloak, 3. ring)
   I will lie to my parents,
   I will say I went over the bridge and
   The wind blew my hat off.

93

INDONESIA

This song is in the form of a **pantun**, an old type of poem in which the first two lines have no relation to the rest of the song and are merely there to create the rhythm of the song. In this type of song the following lines, which may be humorous or satirical, are made up on the spot and can refer to people present. This type of folk song is not related to authentic Indonesian music but is the result of the influence of the music of Western nations which formerly colonised Indonesia. This explains its use of European key structure and the guitar accompaniment.

BARUNG KAKAKTUA

Bu - rung ka-kak tu - a hing - gap di jen - de - la Ne-
nek su-dah tu - a gi - gi - nya ting-gal du - a Tre-
dung tre-dung tre-dung tra la la Tre - dung tre-dung tre - dung tra la la Tre-
dung tre-dung tre - dung tra la la Bu - rung ka-kak tu - a

SOUTH AMERICA

Notice how this folk tune is very repetitive both in rhythms and melodic ideas. The variation used by performers of this piece is to play it three times, each time getting faster. The second section, bars 9 to 12, is the same as the beginning transposed up a fourth.

Authentically this would be played on pan pipes for the melody, guitarrone (a large acoustic bass guitar) for the bass line and a bombo (large dull bass drum) for the rhythm ostinato.

Play 3 times 1) Slow 2) Moderately Fast 3) Very Fast

Revision questions

1. What is folk music?
2. What is meant by 'aural tradition'?
3. What function did the songs of the travelling minstrels serve in the Middle Ages?
4. Who were the troubadours?
5. Name three composers in the 19th century and three from the 20th century who used folk music influences in their works.
6. What is the difference between Magyar and 'gypsy music'?
7. What is a spiritual?
8. What type of folk music flourished in the 1960s in America?
9. Name two performers in this style and give an example of each person's work.
10. Why is folk music a popular style for women performers? Name two.

(For answers, see page 130.)

Worksheet 6

Use this sheet to study and analyse folk songs of your own choice.

Title of song	
Name of performer	
Country of origin	
Date (approximate)	
Describe the vocal style (eg rough/polished/trained/untrained/nasal/operatic/ harsh/emotional/stirring etc).	
List any vocal devices used (eg falsetto/trills/bends/glides/decorations etc).	
Where and how were these devices used?	
List the accompanying instruments.	
What is the style of accompaniment?	

Describe the harmonies (chords) used (eg simple/complex/basic/ unaccompanied/chromatic etc).	
Is the tempo slow/fast/moderate?	
What is the theme of the song?	

Listening

Find some examples of composed music that incorporate folk songs. Complete the following table.

Composer	Work	Type of work/ form, if relevant	Forces used (orchestration, instrumentation)	Folk elements

Suggested listening

Folk influence

Franz Liszt — *Hungarian Rhapsodies*
Johannes Brahms — Hungarian Dances
Edvard Grieg — *Norwegian Dances*
Frédéric Chopin — Polonaises and Mazurkas
Louis Gottschalk — *Bamboula* (uses Negro tunes), *La Bananier, La Savane, Ojos Criollos, Chanson Nègre, Ballade Créole*
Bedřich Smetana — *The Moldau, The Bartered Bride*
Pyotr Tchaikovsky — *The Nutcracker Suite* (trepak), *Swan Lake* (Czardas and Mazurka)
Charles Ives — *Concord Sonata, Putnam's Camp*
Aaron Copland — *Appalachian Spring, Billy the Kid, Rodeo*
Ralph Vaughan Williams — *Fantasia on 'Greensleeves', English Folk Song Suite*
Percy Grainger — 'Molly on the Shore', 'Londonderry Air', 'Scotch Strathspey and Reel', 'Let's Dance Gay in Green Meadow'
Béla Bartók — *Hungarian Folksongs, Romanian Folk Dances, Hungarian Peasant Songs*
Zoltán Kodály — *Háry János Suite*
Manuel de Falla — *The Three-Cornered Hat*
Isaac Albéniz — *Tango, Spanish Suite*
Georges Bizet — 'Habanera' from *Carmen*
Marie-Joseph Canteloube — *Chants d'Auvergne*
Heitor Villa-Lobos — *Suite Populaire Brasilienne*
Leoš Janáček — *Lachian Dances*

Some folk performers

Bob Dylan
Pete Seeger
Woody and Arlo Guthrie
Joan Baez
Judy Collins
Janis Ian
Carole King
The Bushwackers

Buffy St Maree
Joni Mitchell
Tracy Chapman
Suzanne Vega
Redgum
Eric Bogle
The Larrikins

AUSTRALIAN MUSIC

Aboriginal Music

Music is an important aspect of traditional Aboriginal life. It is through music, both song and dance, that the Aborigines learn about their relationship to the land; their environment and how to live in it; their culture and customs; and the way their world was created — the Dreamtime.

Aboriginal ceremonies that combine song and dance are called corroborees — derived from the Aboriginal word 'carib-berie' which meant 'dance' in the language of one of the New South Wales' Aboriginal tribes. Early illustrations show that corroborees were traditionally danced by men with painted bodies who carried shields and weapons. They were accompanied by singers who also provided various rhythms by clapping or beating sticks or boomerangs together. The didgeridoo was occasionally used as the accompanying instrument by southern tribes, however it was most popular, and its use most widespread, across the 'top end' of Australia.

Other Aboriginal tribes have their own dialect name for the corroboree (bora) and each tribe has its own individual dances, songs, singing style and accompaniments. The areas which had the highest numbers of Aborigines (far north Queensland, Northern Territory and Western Australia) produced music with the most diversity.

Corroborees are important in the Aboriginal culture and lifestyle as it is through these song and dance ceremonies that all important events are celebrated — fertility, birth, death, mourning, initiation and the contact the Aborigines have with their ancestors and the supernatural.

Some of these ceremonies are 'open' and can be viewed and participated in by all, whereas others, thought to be too sacred and powerful to be observed and participated in, are 'closed' except to the initiated few. Some corroborees are made up of both open and closed sections.

Corroborees usually begin after sunset and continue throughout the night. The bodies of those taking part are painted and decorated to represent gods or animals. Sometimes the markings are secret and mystical. The bodies of the participants glow in the light of the fires as they dance. Corroborees can be said to be a kind of music theatre of the Aboriginal people.

Questions

1. Why is music important to the Aboriginal people?
2. What does the word corroboree mean?
3. What is meant by comparing corroborees to music theatre?
   (For answers, see page 131.)

Research

1. Find and read an Aboriginal legend from the Dreamtime. Can you put it in your own words? What does it tell you about Aboriginal beliefs?
2. Didgeridoos and other Aboriginal artefacts are often beautifully decorated with symbols and designs. Find an example of Aboriginal design and reproduce it. Does your example have any meaning or is it purely decorative?
3. Investigate Aboriginal art and try and make your own designs using its ideas.

THE MUSIC

A corroboree is made up of a series of short songs (some lasting only a minute or less) with each song accompanied by a dance. Each song in the cycle can vary in the range of notes used, the melody and its accompaniment and the thematic material.

The songs and dances of the Aboriginal people have been handed down through hundreds of generations (and thousands of years) not through written symbols but by rote and imitation of the elders. Many songs and dances are so 'powerful' in their magic and tribal links that they must be performed exactly as they were learnt. In this way songs and dances within the Aboriginal culture have been preserved unchanged throughout the aeons.

Aboriginal music is mainly vocal, or sung, and accompaniments, whether rhythmic or pitched, are minimal. Musical differences occur between tribes and geographical areas, however there are some basic generalisations that can be made about Aboriginal music.

- The voice sings with a nasal quality so it will carry in its out-of-doors performance situation.
- Dynamics do not vary much.
- There is no vibrato in voice production (unlike Western singing).
- The voice is often chant-like.
- The voice often slides between notes of the melody.
- Repeated notes within a song are often ornamented (or varied in some way).
- Melodies are not based on scales or harmonies (as in Western music).
- Aboriginal songs have several pitch centres.
- The melody usually moves from the higher pitch centre to the lower (that is, descending melodies).
- Melodies are undulatory (similar to the Australian landscape).
- Movement by step is common rather than by leap — the music is not angular.
- The 'tonic' is often the final note.
- The melody can be accompanied by the didgeridoo but be independent of its pitch.
- Because of vocal style and performance demands, phrases are often long and good sustained breath control is highly regarded.
- The pitch range of songs varies from as narrow as two notes to greater than an octave.
- Central Australian Aboriginal songs are often made up of many repetitions of a small melodic fragment. The technical term for this is 'iterative'.
- Central Australian songs tend to be accompanied by idiophones only.
- Songs of the far northern tribes tend to be more varied melodically.
- Songs from the north have more varied accompaniments (they use both idiophones as well as aerophones (didgeridoo) and membranophones than do those from southern tribes.
- Group singing is usually in unison.
- Melodic and canonic effects can occur within songs if one singer moves to another pitch centre. Rhythms can also vary between singers, even though they may be singing the same song.

Research

Find out what these musical words mean:

dynamics	pitch range
vibrato	iterative
melody	unison
harmony	canon
scale	octave

Listening

Listen to an example of Aboriginal music and answer the following questions.
1. Graphically notate (draw) the basic shape of the melody.

100

2. What sort of voice/s did you hear? Describe its quality.
3. Was there a pulse? What instrument provided the pulse?
4. Was there any rhythmic accompaniment? What was it played on?
5. Did the melody or tune have any decoration?
6. What instruments did you hear apart from the voice? How did they enter? What was their order of finishing?

Scenes from a corroboree

THE INSTRUMENTS

Aborigines use the resource of their landscape to make their musical instruments. The voice is the most important sound in Aboriginal music though it is usually accompanied in some way.

The most common accompaniment is provided by idiophones:
- handclapping and body slapping
- clap sticks or rhythm sticks. One is usually made of a hard wood and is usually long and flat, the other is of lighter wood and more rounded in shape. When struck together they produce a bright, metallic sound. The rhythm is usually regular and pulse-like
- boomerangs — can be clapped together or rattled
- sticks — can also be beaten against a shield, a bark bundle or on the ground
- didgeridoo — is often tapped on its side by the player

Less common idiophones (found mainly in the North) include:
- rasps
- rattles (made from seed pods, used only by Cape York tribes)
- log drums
- bull roarer — a wooden board swung around on the end of a string. Its sound represents the supernatural and is usually only heard in 'closed' men-only rites.

Membranophones (headed drums) are found only in the music of the Cape York tribes. Their use was probably introduced through contact with the islanders of nearby Melanesia.

The transitory lifestyle and the absence of usable natural materials probably explains why drums are so infrequently used by other Australian Aborigines.

The instrument most commonly associated with Aboriginal music is the didgeridoo, an aerophone. It was traditionally found only in Arnhem Land and possibly Cape York. It is formed from a branch or trunk of a Eucalypt tree that has been hollowed out by termites, cut to a length of between one and two metres, stripped of any bark, and the cracks sealed with beeswax. The mouth or blowing end is about 120 to 130 centimetres wide and is further smoothed and coated with more beeswax. Sometimes mud or a shell is put in this end to help maintain the pressure when blown. The other end is slightly flared. Once made and painted, it is often kept in a stream to preserve its soft tone.

The didgeridoo is blown with vibrating lips and the constant rhythmic drone is maintained by the method of circular or continuous breathing. This technique requires the inhaling of air through the nose while at the same time pushing air from the lungs by squeezing the stomach muscles in. The cheeks are used as a reservoir for the air.

The didgeridoo can produce up to nine notes, but usually there are only two tones produced, a tenth apart. Vocal sounds can also be made through the didgeridoo such as hums, squarks, gurgles and imitations of bird and animal calls. Its drone is unmistakable but it is also capable of producing complicated and changing rhythmic and pitched patterns.

In a performance the rhythm sticks and didgeridoo usually start and finish first, leaving the voice to finish alone.

Questions

1. What are the most common accompanying instruments?
2. What is the long, continuous sound produced by the didgeridoo called?
3. Can you name some other instruments that produce a similar sound? (Hint: Scotland, India.)
4. What could be the reasons for drums not being used in Aboriginal music?
5. What is the most important sound in Aboriginal music?

(For answers, see page 131.)

Listening

Listen to some Aboriginal music. What instruments did you hear? Describe their sound and role. Complete the following table:

Instrument	Sound	Role
1. Voice		
2.		
3.		
4.		

ABORIGINAL SONGS

Traditional Aboriginal songs can be classified into several categories according to their subject matter and how they are performed.

- Children's songs have a similar role to the nursery songs of Western children. They are basically learning songs which tell about the environment and how to live in it.
- Women's songs usually have a social role, such as mourning, fertility and love-magic. They are often sung in a high pitched voice and the phrases are long and ornate.
- Men's songs are often for 'closed' performance only. There are a great many of these.
- Cult songs usually have something to do with the Dreamtime, ancient gods or ancestors of the Aborigines. These songs vary between tribes.
- Clan songs belong to specific family groups and are handed down from father to son. They are often improvised upon.

Many Aboriginal songs and the dances that accompany them are handed down without variation, especially the more important ones, as they are believed to have powerful magical importance. With the changes that have occurred within the Aboriginal culture since white occupation many of the traditional songs have been lost forever. Many Aborigines have turned to and adapted Western styles of music and song.

Country and western songs are in many ways closely related to traditional Aboriginal music. Both country and western songs (usually ballads) and traditional Aboriginal songs tell stories relevant to Aboriginal life. Country and western songs have simple melodic lines and chord progressions which are easy to pick up by a people whose own music is without harmonies.

Students and staff from the Centre for Aboriginal Studies in Music perform "Urban Corroboree" at the Aboriginal Rock Music Festival in Darwin, 1989.

Protest and political songs are also popular for similar reasons and, perhaps more importantly, because of the message they express — and with which the Aboriginal identifies — the depression and oppression the white occupiers have forced upon the Aborigines.

Rock music has been taken to heart especially by the younger generation, partly because of urbanisation but also because the driving, heavy rhythms and volume are seen as more appropriate to getting their message across than the softer folk styles. Furthermore, Aborigines can identify with black cultures around the world through rock styles, such as reggae (from the West Indies) and rhythm and blues (associated with American blacks). Many Aboriginal rock groups use the didgeridoo not only for its unique and identifiable tone colour but for its symbolism of a disenchanted people. White rock groups and melds of white and Aboriginal have also used the didgeridoo (Midnight Oil and Warumpi Band, for instance).

THE INFLUENCE OF ABORIGINAL MUSIC ON OTHER MUSIC

The music of the Australian Aboriginal has also had an effect on contemporary white music. As Australia developed towards independence from Britain, throughout this century, a growing feeling of nationalism developed and people from all the arts turned to Aboriginal culture for inspiration. These first attempts at using Aboriginal elements in literature, poetry and music have been given the name Jindyworobakism. This name was chosen by the poet Rex Ingamells in the 1930s, firstly because it was an authentic Aboriginal name (Jindy-Worobak) and secondly because it meant 'to join' or 'annexe'. In his writing and that of the people from the fields of poetry, literature and music that followed his lead, an attempt was made to blend Aboriginal and English traditions.

Musically, composers in this movement attempted to imitate or recreate Aboriginal melodies and tone colours as well as portraying the Australian landscape and sounds of the Australian bush. The changes and breakthroughs that were happening in Europe at the time with developments in rhythm and atonality gave added impetus to the Australian composers. Probably the most celebrated example of Jindyworobakism in music is *Corroboree* (1946–1950) by John Anthill. He uses instruments to imitate the sounds of clapping sticks and didgeridoo, and tries to use Aboriginal modes, melodic patterns and rhythmic structure.

Some other early attempts at Jindyworobakism include:
- Margaret Sutherland — *Haunted Hills* (1950), the opera *The Young Kabbarli* (1965) based on the life of Western woman Daisy Bates and her life among the Aborigines of Western Australia. By texture and tone colour Sutherland attempted to portray the sparseness of the Australian bush.
- Clive Douglas — *Kaditch* (1938), *Carwoola* (1939).
- James Pemberty — *Kadjani and Julunggal* (1957), *The Earth Mother* (1958).

Recent Australian composers have been more successful in their attempts to merge Western and Aboriginal music as well as in their portrayals of the Australian landscape. Included among these composers are:
- Peter Sculthorpe — *Sun Music I–IV, Irkanda IV, Rites of Passage* (an opera based on the language and ceremonies of the Aranda tribe), *Song of Talitnama* (uses Aboriginal melodies), *String Quartets Nos 6 and 7 (Red Landscape).*
- Richard Meale — *Plateau for Wind Quintet.*
- George Dreyfus — *Sextet for Wind Quintet and Didgeridoo.*
- Colin Bright — *The Dreamtime* (with Aboriginal words), *Music for Contrabass Octet and Didgeridoo.*
- Gondwanaland — a three piece performing group which successfully merges the tone colours and rhythms of the didgeridoo with the mysterious yet distinctly 20th century sound of synthesisers.

Questions

1. What do traditional Aboriginal songs have in common with country and western music?
2. Why are Aborigines attracted to listening and performing rock music?
3. What does the term Jindyworobakism mean?
4. Name the first important work, and its composer, that included elements of Aboriginal music (like tone colour and feel).
5. Name one contemporary Australian composer and a work that is influenced by Aboriginal music or the Australian landscape.

(For answers, see page 131.)

Listening

1. Listen to some modern Aboriginal performers or groups and then complete this table.

Name of performer/group	Song title	Style or type of song	Aboriginal elements

2. Listen to an example of contemporary music that has Aboriginal or Australian influences. Complete this table.

Name of work	Composer	Aboriginal or Australian influences (eg effects, tone colour, instruments)

Some discussion topics

- What contemporary issues concern Aborigines in our society today?
- Are these issues being voiced in their music?
- Do Aboriginal rock groups get enough air-play? If not, why not?
- Have you seen any Aboriginal performing group (either singing or dancing)?
- If so, can you describe the impact it made on you?
- If you haven't seen an Aboriginal group perform, why do you think this might be so?

Art Music — An Historical Overview

The beginnings and much of the history of art music in Australia are dominated by European influence. This is not surprising considering the colonisation process and the need for composers to study overseas until the late 20th century. Music in the early colonial situation was important for military, religious, and social occasions, and composers soon began writing music for these. Often these were given distinctive Australian titles, for example in the 1840s William Ellard wrote a set of *Australian Quadrilles* with the titles 'La Sydney', 'La Wooloomooloo' [sic], 'La Illawara' [sic], 'La Bong Bong', and 'La Engelhurst'. These however turned out to be not original pieces but arrangements of popular tunes of the day; 'La Sydney', for instance, using the march from Act I of Bellini's *Norma*.

Early Australian compositions often used this practice of titles with reference to colonial life, and ballads, songs and marches were given such names as 'The Trumpet Sounds Australia's Fame' and 'General Ralph Darling's Australian Slow March', but the music was written in the style popular in England at the time.

The first acknowledged Australian composer was Isaac Nathan (UK 1790–Sydney 1864) who made a point of studying Aboriginal music and incorporating some of its melodies into his own music. Nathan is credited with the first opera to be written and performed in Australia, *Don John of Austria* (1847).

Around the turn of the 19th century there appeared two Australians who are considered to be Australia's first famous composers, Alfred Hill and Percy Grainger. Alfred Hill (1870–1960) was important as both a composer and teacher, being Professor of Composition at the New South Wales State Conservatorium from 1915 to 1934. His music, written in late 19th century idiom, often uses programmatic titles some of which are specifically Australian, such as *Australia* (*Symphony No 3*).

Percy Grainger

106

Grainger (1882–1961) was a child prodigy who later became a concert pianist, as well as composer, conductor, writer and teacher. His music, although harmonically not forward thinking and similar to that of his English contemporaries, shows his own brand of avant-garde ideas. For example, he invented a number of instruments, some made from junk and disused machines; he advocated the orchestral use of unusual instruments, like the banjo and mouth organ; he included the piano as an orchestral instrument; he saw Asian percussion instruments as an important influence; and he scored his music so it could be played on any number of convenient instruments (he called this 'elastic scoring'). He collected many folk songs, many of which he arranged. It is a pity that he is most remembered by these instead of his own original compositions.

Both Hill and Percy Grainger demonstrate the same need in their early training — they both had to leave Australia to study overseas. Hill studied in Leipzig, and Grainger in Berlin. This was the common method in those days of becoming a serious musician.

As the 20th century progressed the need to study overseas, though still strong, lessened with the arrival in Australia of recognised composers who took up positions here. A good example of this is Eugene Goossens (1893–1962), an English composer and conductor who became director of the New South Wales State Conservatorium in 1947 and had among his composition pupils Ron Grainer (b1923) who wrote the theme music for 'Dr Who' and 'Steptoe and Son', and Malcolm Williamson (b1931) who became Master of the Queen's Music in 1975.

At the same time there was an increasing attempt to create an Australian music style. This is seen in one of the most famous orchestral works of the 1940s, the ballet *Corroboree* by John Antill (1904–1987). His interest in Aboriginal music led Antill to imitate the sounds of its instruments in his orchestral writing, but this is not his only composition worth hearing. He is perhaps one of the most important composers of this period of Australian music history.

The decades after World War II saw the development of a new group of young composers. They still studied overseas but later took up positions in Australian universities and conservatoria, and thus the teaching of composition became distinctly Australian, with its own pupils and products. Among these composers are Peter Sculthorpe (b1929), Nigel Butterley (b1935) and Colin Brumby (b1933). Other famous Australian composers of the same time are George Dreyfus (b1928), Clive Douglas (1903–1977), Larry Sitsky (b1934), and Richard Meale (b1932).

Composer, Peter Sculthorpe

David Malouf (librettist) and Richard Meale (composer) during a rehearsal of Voss.

With these composers there is talk of the emergence of an 'Australian style' of composition, though this is always hard to define. Probably what people mean is that with this group of composers working at the same time and passing their ideas on to other composers, a large amount of music was produced where previously there had been very little, and this music looked like the beginning of a new style. These composers are also recognised worldwide and this was also a new situation for so many Australian composers.

In the last quarter of the 20th century the field of composition in Australia has developed tremendously. This has been due to a number of factors and has also shown a number of musical influences. Among the factors helping this development has been the teaching of composition by such musicians as Peter Sculthorpe. Also important is government funding administered through the Australia Council. Performing bodies and entrepreneurial boards have created demands for Australian compositions, and the Bicentenary celebrations gave rise to a lot of Australian music, written for celebrations and competitions.

The musical influences that can be seen in Australian composition in the late 20th century include Asian music (*Sun Music III* by Sculthorpe), electronic music (the music of Martin Wesley-Smith, b1945), jazz (pianist/composer Mike Nock), the invention of new instruments (in the music of Ros Bandt), and ethnic music reflecting the mixed racial background of Australia (for example in the music of twin brothers Christos and Tassos Ioannidis). There is also a new group of composers developing, including opera composer Brian Howard (b1951), Nigel Westlake (b1958), Carl Vine (b1955), Vincent Plush (b1950), and Michael Smetanin (b1958).

Stuart Challender (conductor), Jim Sharman (director), Chrissie Koltai (choreographer), Brian Thomson (set designer), Luciana Arrighi (costume designer) and David Malouf (librettist) watch a rehearsal of Voss.

Revision questions

1. What were the uses of music in early colonial Australia?
2. What was the common practice for naming musical works in early Australian music?
3. Who was the first acknowledged Australian composer? Name a work by him. What was his attitude to Aboriginal music?
4. Who were the first two famous Australian composers? What did they have in common?
5. What was typically Australian about Hill's music?
6. What were Grainger's avant-garde ideas?
7. Who were two of Goossens' famous pupils?
8. What work by Antill is famous for its attempts at recreating Aboriginal sounds?
9. Who are three composers who also teach?
10. Why has composition developed so much in the last quarter of the 20th century?
11. What influences can be seen in late 20th century Australian music?

(For answers, see page 131.)

Activities

1. Many pieces of contemporary Australian music have been written especially for performance by school pupils. Perform some of these in class.
2. Select one Australian composer for study. Research this composer's life and music, listen to his or her music and analyse it. Is there anything distinctly Australian about the music? What influences can you hear in the music?
3. Select one composer from each of the following historical areas:
   (a) colonial and early 20th century
   (b) mid-20th century
   (c) post-1945
   (d) last quarter of the 20th century.
   Listen to music by each one and fill in the following worksheet for each composer.

Worksheet 7

Composer	Dates
Historical area	
Music example	
Style	
Instrumentation	
What elements make this Australian?	
What musical influences are there in the work?	

Jazz in Australia

By the 1980s, jazz had become a recognised part of Australian music with its own stars, venues, tertiary courses, influences, and, as some see it, distinctive sound. To reach that stage, however, it went through periods of development, and two declines in popularity. A convenient place to divide the history of jazz in Australia into two sections is World War II.

BEFORE WORLD WAR II

Jazz, being an American style of music, could not be spread unless groups from America visited Australia, musicians travelled to America to hear them, or American recordings were heard in Australia. In the last years of the 19th century Negro minstrel groups toured the east coast of Australia and by the 1920s these had been replaced by jazz groups, such as Sonny Clay's Colored Idea who toured in 1928. Other contacts with Americans, including the 1908 visit of the Great Fleet and contacts with troops during World War I, had paved the way and created interest in what was then a new style of music. The new technology of sound recordings provided the main source of jazz inspiration and was the most important factor contributing to the spread of jazz throughout Australia. The release of 'Lazy Daddy' in 1921 by the Original Dixieland Jazz Band, the first American jazz recording issued in Australia, was a landmark event in the history of jazz in this country.

Australians did have their own jazz bands before they heard much imported American jazz, but their names and instrumental lineups (including violin) imply music more like foxtrots and two-steps (salon dance music) rather than blues-based New Orleans style improvised jazz; Miss Nellie McEwan's Jazz Quartette (trombone, flute, piano, violin, and drums), for instance.

The American bands that visited Australia were very popular and of course musicians began to appreciate the jazz characteristics of their music and to change their own sound. Violins were discarded and the more genteel style of brass playing, which was probably a carry over from the brass band style where many players had been trained, was gradually replaced by the stronger style we associate with real jazz.

In the 1920s and 1930s, dance halls were the main jazz venues — famous dance halls included Melbourne's Green Mill, and the Sydney Palais Royal. The other performance possibility was the theatre circuit, jazz bands being contracted to tour, for example, the Tivoli theatres in capital cities. Australian groups from this time include Art Chapman's Band, Tom Swift's Green Mill Orchestra, Eric Pearse and his Astoria Band, and Joe Aronson's Band (he was known as the Rajah of jazz).

What these bands played was influenced by American jazz, but the lack of real contact with jazz's originators meant that they played their own music and jazz versions of popular songs. By the early 1930s, however, Australia did have its own jazz oriented magazine.

With the spread of gramophone records and radio broadcasts in the 1930s, the influence of the new swing style from America was felt and was seen in the increase in size of jazz groups. The new musical style was taken up by such groups as Jay Whidden's Palaise de Dance Band and Frank Coughlan's Trocadero Orchestra. Notice that like the famous American bands of this era, they were named after their leader, and were still linked very strongly to a dance tradition and venue.

AFTER WORLD WAR II

When musicians rejoined groups they had left because of the war, there was a strong influence from the contact they had had with Americans both in war locations and at home in Australia (remember Australia was used as a rest and recreation location by the American forces in the Pacific). This influence was immediately seen in the emergence of bop, the new style of jazz in the 1940s which was briefly popular alongside the swing style.

The 1940s is most noteworthy as the decade that gave rise to the beginnings of an Australian jazz style. These beginnings can be located in the work of Graeme Bell, one of Australia's most important jazz performers. At the time, there was an intermingling of radical ideas from the fields of music, painting, literature and politics, and Bell and his circle were at the centre of the resulting cultural movement.

Graeme Bell All Stars

During the 1950s we can see the further development of Australian jazz that was to lead to the 1980s. By this time, many Australian jazz musicians who were later to become famous had already established their careers. These include Bobby Limb (tenor sax), Bob Gibson (band leader), Errol Buddle (sax and bassoon), Charlie Munro (sax) and Don Burrows (sax and flute etc).

Another important development of this period was the cross-fertilisation of jazz with 'serious' composition. This is best seen in the music of the late composer Don Banks (1923–1980) who, originally classically trained, had his own jazz group called the Don Banks Boptet, and wrote music that shows a heavy jazz influence; *Blues for Two* is a good example.

Until the mid-1960s, Australian jazz developed and produced many important performers. Graeme Bell's career was already well under way and he continued as a prominent recording and performing artist. He preferred a traditional style of jazz rather than the modern types favoured by artists such as John Sangster (vibes etc), also important as a jazz composer.

From about 1964 to the mid-1970s, jazz, though it has always had its supporters, seemed to wane in popularity. This was initially due to the advent of The Beatles and later to the onslaught of the 1970s rock groups and the beginnings of the Australian rock industry. In the 1980s, however, there has been a resurgence of interest in jazz, shown by the successes of performers such as Vince Jones, Kate Ceberano, Roger Frampton and James Morrison.

In the 1980s Australian jazz shows a number of style influences from all types of jazz — New Orleans to modern, to rock influenced, even reggae influenced. Some people see Australian jazz as distinct from American jazz and say it has its own sound, though they find it difficult to explain what this sound is. What we do know is that Australia has a jazz tradition which has produced many important musicians who have had success both in Australia and overseas.

Don Burrows

James Morrison

Vince Jones

Australian jazz and popular music vocalist, Kate Ceberano

Revision questions

1. How did Australians find out about early jazz?
2. Name the jazz group that toured to Australia in 1928.
3. How did Australian groups differ from American groups originally?
4. What differences took place musically after Australians had heard a number of American groups?
5. What two types of venues did people visit to hear jazz in the 1920s and 1930s?
6. What technological advances helped spread jazz in the 1930s?
7. Explain why Australians had so much contact with Americans during World War II.
8. Which Australian composer combined classical and jazz music in compositions such as *Blues for Two*?
9. Why did jazz seem to decline in popularity from the mid-1960s to the mid-1970s?
10. List four important jazz performers of the 1970s onwards.

(For answers, see page 132.)

Activities

1. Listen to pieces of Australian jazz. Differentiate between covers of American originals and original Australian pieces.
2. Collect newspaper and magazine articles on Australian jazz and performers.

Worksheet 8

Select Australian jazz performers from before World War II, after the war, and the 1980s. Listen to music by each one and fill in the following worksheet for each piece.

Title of piece	
Date **Performer**	
Original writer	
Style of jazz	
Is this Australian or a cover of an American piece?	
What elements in the piece make it Australian?	
How does it differ from American jazz?	
Name the performers and their instruments.	

Australian Popular Music

Originally Australian popular music followed trends set in America and Britain. Songs in the 1930s and 1940s were written in the style of the then standard 32 bar pattern and used the general swing jazz style that was in vogue at that time. After World War II, the situation continued — when rock groups became popular in America and later England, Australia had rock groups; when folk music was the important influence in the 1960s, Australia developed a folk scene and had groups such as The Seekers. It was not until the 1970s that the Australian rock industry developed into an independent force within Australian popular music.

This development was linked to the 1970s promotion of an Australian identity and the resultant widespread demand to hear Australian groups. In the larger cities, the rock scene was boosted by developments in the recording industry, the creation of the pub rock circuit (in an attempt to attract customers) and the popularity of live music. By the 1980s the rock group scene in Australia was recognised as producing some of the best rock music in the world with groups such as Midnight Oil, Men at Work, and the Little River Band making successful tours of America — still considered by many bands to be an important career move.

As well as rock music, there are also the performers of pop music. Because pop music changes and fashions vary so quickly, it is hard to see 'stars' who have long success rates. One of the most famous of the late 1980s is Kylie Minogue ('Do the Locomotion') who has received worldwide fame.

Kylie Minogue

A thriving country music scene is also part of Australian popular music. This too has its own mega-stars and its own annual awards at Tamworth. Important personalities in this music are Slim Dusty ('The Pub With No Beer'), Olivia Newton-John, who started out as a country singer and now owns a boutique in Los Angeles, and John Williamson ('Every Australian Boy Needs a Shed', 'True Blue' and 'Rip, Rip, Woodchip').

Overseas, Australian popular artists include Peter Allen, who is not only a performer but also composer of songs such as 'Tenterfield Saddler' and 'I Still Call Australia Home'.

Here is the music for a song from the group Men at Work. 'Down Under' was a big hit for them both here and overseas in 1981. Unusually for a rock group they included a flute in their lineup for this song. Notice the references to Australia (the land down under) and to things only Australians would understand: Vegemite, and 'chunder' (= to vomit). Except for two bars at the end of the chorus, this song is built over a bass ostinato two bars long. It uses the standard rock pattern of verse–chorus repeated a number of times.

DOWN UNDER

Words and Music by Colin Hay and Ron Strykert

Tra-vel-ling in a fried out com - bie he was
Buy-ing bread from a man in Brus - sels
Ly-ing in a den in Bom - bay

on a hip-py trail, head full of zom - bie.
six foot four and full of mus-cles.
with a slack jaw and much to say.

CHORUS - (to fade out)

1.3 "Do you come from a land down un - der._____
2. "I come from a land down un - der._____

118

where wo-men glow___ and men plun - der?
where beer does flow___ and men chun - der.

Can't you hear, can't you hear the thun - der?_____   You
Can't you hear, can't you hear the thun - der?_____   You

bet-ter run_____ you bet-ter take_____ co - ver."_____
bet-ter run_____ you bet-ter take_____ co - ver."_____

D.S. to fade

120

Revision questions

1. The music of which countries did early Australian popular music imitate?
2. When did Australian rock music start to develop on its own?
3. Name three groups that successfully toured overseas.
4. What was the name of Kylie Minogue's worldwide hit?
5. In what style of music did Olivia Newton-John start her career?
6. Who wrote 'I Still Call Australia Home'?
7. How long is the bass guitar ostinato in 'Down Under'?
8. What group had a hit with 'Down Under'?
9. What unusual instrument was used in 'Down Under'?
10. What typical pattern is used to construct the song 'Down Under'?

(For answers, see page 132.)

Listening

Listen to examples of Australian popular music and fill in the information needed in this table.

Song	Performer	Date	Style	What is typically Australian about the song?

Australian Folk Music

The Australian folk tradition has its roots in the music of England and more particularly Ireland. While many convicts sent to Australia in the 18th century were illiterate, petty criminals from the overcrowded English prisons, a great number were politically active Irish who the British government sent to Australia to 'get out of the way'. These Irish brought with them the tunes of their native land as well as their passion for equality and distrust of 'the bosses' and their English overlords. The link between folk music and political protest has remained part of the Australian music tradition ever since.

Australian folk music gives important information about the settlement of Australia and its growth and development into nationhood. Different songs can be related to groups of people that either came to Australia to start new lives as immigrants or were sent as convicts. The first folk songs were probably about transport to Australia, for example, 'Botany Bay', 'Ten Thousand Miles Away' and 'The Girl with the Black Velvet Band'. Later songs often tell about the appalling conditions and hardship the convicts suffered, for example in the songs 'Jim Jones' and 'Moreton Bay'.

'Moreton Bay' is a mournful, hauntingly beautiful Irish tune, but the lyrics tell a story of the terrible penal institutions and their overseers. The Captain Logan spoken of in the song was a notorious tyrant who treated convicts with extreme cruelty. The song likens the convict system to the injustices of slavery, and provides a powerful example of folk music.

MORETON BAY

tore me from my ___ a - ged par - ents and from the mai-den whom I do a - dore".

2. I've been a prisoner at Port Macqurie, at Norfolk Island and Emu Plains
   at Castle Hill and at curs'd Toongabbie and at those settlements I've worked in chains.
   But of all the places of condemnation and penal stations of New South Wales
   To Moreton Bay I have found no equal, excessive tyranny each day prevails.

3. For three long years I was beastly treated and heavy irons on my legs I wore
   My back with flogging is lacerated and often pained with my crimson gore.
   And many men downright starvation lay mouldering now underneath the clay
   And Captain Logan he had us mangled at the triangles of Moreton Bay.

4. Like the Egyptians and ancient Hebrews we were oppressed under Logan's yoke
   Till a native lying there in ambush did give our tyrant his mortal stroke.
   My fellow prisoners be exhilarated that all such monsters such a death may find
   And when from bondage we are liberated our former sufferings may fade from mind.

The settlers and their battle against the harshness of the land are represented by songs such as 'The Limejuice Tub' which is about shearing, 'The Drover's Dream' and 'The Dying Stockman'. The struggle of the 'cocky' battling the hardships of the land continues today and is described in such modern songs as 'Now I'm Easy' by Eric Bogle.

Bushrangers are mentioned in many songs, including 'The Wild Colonial Boy', the 'Ballad of Ben Hall', 'Bold Jack Donoghue' and 'Ned Kelly'. Many of these songs kept alive the rebellious spirit of the Irish and the battle between the government and the struggling settler. The goldrushes in the early to mid-19th century are represented in songs like 'With My Swag All on My Shoulder'.

Significant political events often found their way into song — 'Eureka Stockade' and the 'Ballad of 1891' are two good examples. There are also songs about freedom and rebellion in general, such as 'Freedom on the Wallaby', in which words by the Australian poet Henry Lawson are set to music.

FREEDOM ON THE WALLABY

1. Aus - tra - li - a's a big coun - try and free-dom's hump - ing blue-ey, An'
Free-dom's on the wal - la - by, Oh can't you hear 'er coo - ey? She's

just be-gun to boom - er - ang. She'll knock the tyr - ants sil - ly, She's

go-ing to light an - oth - er fire And boil an - oth - er bil - ly.

2. Our fathers toiled for bitter bread
   While loafers thrived beside 'em,
   But food to eat and clothes to wear,
   Their native land denied them.
   And so they left that native land,
   In spite of their devotion,
   And so they came, or if they stole,
   Were sent across the ocean.

3. Our fathers grubbed to make a home,
   Hard grubbin' t'was and clearin',
   They wasn't troubled much with lords
   When they was pioneerin'.
   But now that we have made this land
   A garden full of promise,
   Old Greed must crook 'is ugly hand
   An' come ter take it from us.

4. So we must fly the rebel flag
   As others did before us,
   And we must sing a rebel song
   And join in rebel chorus.
   We'll make the tyrants feel the sting
   O' those that they would throttle;
   They needn't say the fault is ours
   If blood should stain the wattle.

The tradition of a link between folk song and political comment can be seen in modern folk song compositions and the continuing performance of traditional songs by politically oriented groups. Folk groups such as The Larrikins use many old songs like 'Freedom on the Wallaby' as well as singing new ones about current issues; for example their song 'F1-11' is about the purchase of some very expensive fighter planes that turned out to be inefficient and a waste of money and 'Terania Creek' is about saving the rainforests. This trend can be seen in other songs including Eric Bogle's 'What a Friend We Have in Malcolm' (Malcolm Fraser was a Liberal prime minister in the 1970s); 'Song of the Humpback Whale', about conservation of the whales; Redgum's 'Beaumont Rag', about class distinction in Australia; 'Elizabeth the Last', by Dennis Kevans, which expresses republican sympathies. Through its association with different social causes and movements, folk music has contributed greatly to the public airing of important issues.

Another important feature of Australian folk music is the way it has been used to create a collective identity, a feeling of unity amongst the population of a relatively new settlement. The folk songs of the early years led to a feeling of nationhood, realised at the beginning of this century. The relevance of these songs to the Australian population is the main reason why old folk songs can still be used by modern performers — the topics of the early folk songs are not limited by time, even though references may be made to specific personalities and events that have been forgotten.

The first folk songs were sung unaccompanied, and often in an undertone as 'rebel' songs were considered treasonous and were punished cruelly by floggings or death. As the land was settled instruments began to be used. The harmonica was one of the first instruments because of its portability and poignant tone. Accordions, violins or fiddles, and the penny whistle harked back to Irish roots. Other instruments were made from whatever was at hand — the tea-chest bass, lagerphone, the 'spoons' and comb and paper (kazoo) formed the basis of a 'bush band'. Instruments such as piano or guitars were added if available.

Dancing was an important part of the Australian social life, particularly in the country areas. This tradition survives today, with the B and S (Bachelors and Spinsters) balls held all over the country. Many of the bush dances are of Irish origin, especially the jigs and reels with their

distinctive triplet (♪♪♪ ♪♪♪) or $\frac{6}{8}$ feel. Most are 'set' dances rather than couple dances. Bush

dances have always been popular and there has been a resurgence since the 1970s. The most famous bush dance group was the Bushwackers.

Sirocco

As the origins of the Australian people become more diverse, the Irish 'bush' music tradition is being modified. Groups such as Sirocco are mixing the music of countries in South America, the Mediterranean and the Middle East with music inherited from the Irish and the Australian Aborigines. The result is a new cross-cultural tradition which reflects the multi-cultural nature of Australian society.

Revision questions

1. Give an example of each folk song important in Australia's folk heritage.
   Sea-shanty
   Transport
   Convict
   Settler
   Bushranger
   Goldrush
   Political or 'rebel'
2. Which group of convicts highlighted political themes in their songs?
3. Modern political songs can concern:
   Conservation
   Class distinction
   Republicanism
   Give an example of each kind and the singer/group.
4. What instruments make up a bush band?
5. What is the difference between a 'set' dance and a 'couple' dance?

(For answers, see page 132.)

Listening

Complete the following table from your listening.

Song	Performer	Type of song	Musical features

Answers

Background of jazz

1. Question and answer: a musical device in which phrases alternate with each other — found in African music and blues
2. Pentatonic: music based on a five-note scale — found in African music and also spirituals
3. Cross-rhythm: when different rhythms occur at the same time — common in African music and ragtime
4. Syncopation: the disturbance of the normal accent in music — typical of African music and one of the main features of ragtime
5. Stride playing: a style of piano accompaniment in which the left hand plays octaves on the first and third beats and chords on the off-beats, eg

 — found in ragtime

6. Call and response: musical device in which a soloist (call) is answered by a group (response). Often the call differs each time but the response is the same — typical of African music and spirituals
7. Primary triads, I, IV and V: the principal chords in a key used for basic harmony — used to construct the 12 bar blues pattern
8. Blues: the name of Negro songs expressing unhappiness
9. 12 bar blues: a chord pattern of 12 bars,

   I / I / I / I / IV / IV / I / I / IV / IV / I / I //

   — the basis of blues songs
10. Blue notes: notes purposely at variance with their accompanying harmony — found in blues

'Tuxedo Junction'

1. In the key of A major
2. The repeated A is a pedal or pedal point and it reinforces the key centre
3. Scat or scatting (though in this case the line is not improvised)
4. Bars 3 (treble and bass), 5 (treble and bass), 7 and 8 (treble) are syncopated
5. Putting an accent in an unexpected place or not accenting in an expected place

Sign	Meaning
𝅝 ⌣ 𝅘𝅥	Tied notes — the value of the second is added to the first, but is not played again
♮	Natural sign. It negates the # sign of the key signature in the bar where it occurs
▬	2 beat or minim rest

'Rum and Coca Cola'

1. Binary or two parts
2. Bars 9-10, 11-12, 13-14, 16-17
3. $\frac{4}{4}$ or C common time
4. C major
5.

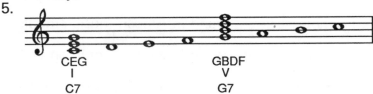

CEG   GBDF
I   V
C7   G7

History of jazz styles

1. Ragtime — Scott Joplin
   Stride — Fats Waller
   Boogie-woogie — Meade 'Lux' Lewis, Clarence 'Pinetops' Smith, Albert Ammons
2. **Dixieland**

Dixieland	**New Orleans**
White style	'Black' style
Less expressive	'Hot' style
Less performance features like sliding, glissandi	Uses glissandi, sliding between notes, vibrato
More orthodox (harmonically and technically)	

3. Louis Armstrong — trumpet   Gene Krupa — drums
   Jelly Roll Morton — piano   Bix Beiderbecke — cornet
4. Large 'big' bands containing three main sections: trumpets, saxophones and trombones
   Less freedom to improvise — arrangements were played
   Used riffs (sectionalised)
   $\frac{4}{4}$ time with an emphasis on each beat
5. Glen Miller — trombone
   Count Basie, Duke Ellington, Luis Russell — piano
   Artie Shaw — clarinet
   Dorsey Brothers: Jimmy Dorsey — sax, clarinet; Tommy Dorsey — trombone
6. Bebop
   Dizzy Gillespie — trumpet
   Charlie Parker — saxophone
7. Traditional jazz — a kind of jazz which became popular in the 1940s as a reaction against bebop
8. Small groups
   Technically brilliant performers
   Complex harmonies and improvisations
   Short melodic fragments put together in a nervous and frenetic way
9. A style of jazz which is a mixture of jazz and classical music
10. Fusion

'Someday My Prince Will Come'

1. $\frac{3}{4}$ or waltz time
2. B♭ major
3.

4. Chords that have more notes in them than the basic triad — this song uses many sevenths
   Makes the sound of the chord richer
5. A chord progression in which the bass notes of the chords are a fifth apart eg C – F – B – E – etc (the last seven bars are a cycle of fifths)
6. G⁷⁺ — A G major triad with the top note raised a semitone to D#, plus an

   added minor seventh (F) = ♯♮ (called an 'augmented G seven')

   E♭ᵒ — a diminished seventh on E♭

7. Chromatic — because it uses many accidentals to flavour the music
8. First and second endings
9. By the use of jazz harmony

Instruments of jazz

1. Drumkit, piano and bass (eg double bass or electric bass)
2. The drummer played a pulse on cymbals rather than on the bass drum while the bass drum played special effects — the free hand played 'counter rhythms' to other performers on remaining drums and cymbals
3. Art Tatum — stride · · · · · · · · · · · Lil Hardin — New Orleans
   Bill Evans — 1950s bebop · · · · · · · Earl Hines — big band (1930s)
   Albert Ammons — boogie-woogie · · Joe Zawinal — fusion (1970s)
   Herbie Hancock — electric (1970s) · Errol Garner — stride
4. *St James Infirmary*
   St Louis Blues
5. Type of large trumpet with a richer sound
   Louis Armstrong
   Miles Davis
6. Saxophone — Charlie 'Bird' Parker
   Clarinet — Sidney Bechet
7. Clarinet — associated with Dixieland
8. (3) tenor — Lester Young, Dexter Gordon
   (4) baritone — Harry Carney
   (2) alto — Charlie Parker, Johnny Hodges
   (1) soprano — Sidney Bechet
9. Violin — Stephane Grapelli
   Flute — Don Burrows
10. A style of jazz singing where the voice imitates instruments, usually using 'nonsense' syllables rather than words

The Influence of Jazz on Other Styles of Music

1. Debussy uses jazz rhythms in *The Golliwogg's Cakewalk*.
   Ravel uses blues-sounding chord progressions in his *Sonata for Piano and Violin*.
   Stravinsky imitates the instrumentation of early jazz groups in *Ragtime for 11 Instruments*.
   Weill uses jazz-like chords and fills in *The Rise and Fall of the City of Mahagonny*.
   Gershwin uses syncopation, blue notes and sections designed to sound like improvisation in *Rhapsody in Blue*.
   Milhaud uses jazz inspired rhythms in his ballets *The Ox on the Roof* and *The Creation of the World*.
2. Debussy and Ravel were art music composers who used touches of jazz style as an unusual device in their work.
   Kurt Weill was a classically trained composer who became a composer of popular music.
   George Gershwin was a symphonic composer who wrote in a jazz style.
3. Gershwin made *Rhapsody in Blue* sound like jazz through his use of blue notes, syncopation and sections designed to sound like improvisation.
4. Leonard Bernstein.
   West Side Story.

Folk music

1. Folk music is music of the 'people' — there is always a feeling of communality or group ownership of the song or music
2. When music is not written down and is handed down aurally, that is, learning by repetition
3. Minstrels brought news from village to village as well as information, songs that bore moral messages and gossip
4. Poet-musicians of noble birth (they were not really part of the folk music tradition)
5. **19th century**   **20th century**
   Liszt, Brahms, Dvorak,   Copeland, Ives,
   Grieg, Smetana,   Grainger,
   Gottschalk, Tchaikovsky   Vaughan Williams
6. Magyar music — the traditional music of Hungary, is often modal, has irregular rhythms and accents
   Gypsy music — gypsies are itinerant peoples found in many countries — Hungarian gypsy music is characterised by lots of decoration and improvisation, abrupt changes in tempo and sudden stops
7. Religious song associated with American blacks — originally sung by the black slaves, they are concerned with life after death
8. Protest songs
9. Bob Dylan — 'A Hard Rain's a'Gonna Fall', 'Mr Tambourine Man'
   Pete Seeger — 'Where Have All the Flowers Gone?'
   Simon and Garfunkel — 'The Sounds of Silence'
10. Folk music is lyrical and acoustic (not amplified) Joan Baez, Buffy St Marie, Tracy Chapman, Suzanne Vega

Aboriginal music

1. Aborigines learn about their relationship to the land, their culture, customs, history and environment through their music
2. Corroboree means 'dance'
3. Corroborees often portray dramatic aspects and stories of the Aboriginal Dreamtime. They combine music, dance and song into a 'theatrical' performance

Instruments
1. Didgeridoo, clapsticks or rhythm sticks, and body percussion
2. Drone
3. Bagpipes, sitars also produce drones (see Folk Music chapter)
4. Not enough available material eg large hard-wood tree trunks; the Aborigines moved about constantly, covering a large amount of territory — drums would have been too heavy to transport
5. The voice

Songs
1. Both tell stories relevant to Aborigines
2. Many Aborigines live in cities (ie are urban) and rock music is relevant to their lives and also the powerful rhythms and amplification are considered appropriate for 'driving' home their message
3. The using of Aboriginal elements in white literature, poetry and music
4. *Corroboree* by John Anthill
5. Peter Sculthorpe — *Irkanda* (among others)

Art music

1. Military, religious, and social occasions
2. Composers used Australian titles
3. Isaac Nathan — *Don John of Austria*
   He researched and used Aboriginal melodies
4. Alfred Hill, Percy Grainger
   They both studied overseas
5. He gave his music programmatic Australian titles
6. He invented instruments; he used unusual instruments in the orchestra; he saw Asian music as an important influence; he scored his music so it could be played on any combination of instruments
7. Ron Grainer, Malcolm Williamson
8. *Corroboree*
9. Peter Sculthorpe, Nigel Butterley, Colin Brumby
10. The teaching of composition by composers, funding from government bodies, the work of performing bodies and entrepreneurial boards, and the Bicentenary celebrations
11. Asian music, electronic music, the invention of new instruments, ethnic music

Jazz in Australia

1. Mostly from visiting groups
2. Sonny Clay's Colored Idea
3. Their music was more like dance music and they used instruments such as the violin
4. Violins were not used, brass playing became stronger
5. Dance halls and theatres
6. Gramophone records and radio
7. They fought alongside them, and Australia was used as a rest and recreation location by the American forces in the Pacific
8. Don Banks
9. Initially because of the advent of The Beatles and later because of the beginnings of the Australian rock industry
10. Vince Jones, Kate Ceberano, Roger Frampton, James Morrison

Australian popular music

1. America and Britain
2. The 1970s
3. Midnight Oil, the Little River Band, Men at Work
4. 'Do the Locomotion'
5. Country
6. Peter Allen
7. 2 bars
8. Men at Work
9. A flute
10. Verse — chorus

Australian folk music

1. Sea Shanty — 'Bound for South Australia'
   Transport — 'Bound for Botany Bay', 'Girl with the Black Velvet Band'
   Convict — 'Moreton Bay'
   Settler — 'Limejuice Tub', 'Dying Stockman'
   Bushranger — 'Bold Jack Donoghue', 'Wild Colonial Boy'
   Goldrush — 'With the Swag All on My Shoulder'
   Political/Rebel — 'Freedom on the Wallaby'
2. The Irish prisoners
3. Conservation: 'Terania Creek' — The Larrikins, 'Song of the Humpback Whale' — Eric Bogle
   Class Distinction: 'Beaumont Rag' — Redgum
   Republicanism: 'Elizabeth the Last' — Denis Kevans
4. Tea chest bass, lagerphone, spoons, guitar, penny whistle, accordion, fiddle or violin
5. Set dance is a group dance whereas a couple dance is made up of pairs of dancers

Glossary

accelerando	gradually getting faster
additive chord	a chord in jazz in which extra notes have been added to the basic triad
aerophone	an instrument which is blown
anticipation	performing a note slightly before it is due
arpeggiation	playing the notes of a chord separately
arrangement	a different version of an original piece of music
atonality	the absence of tonality, not in any key
avant-garde	artistic trends that are ahead of the mainstream
ballad	a song that tells a story
bend	vocal and instrumental effect in which the pitch of a note is altered
binary form	a musical plan with two different sections, AB
blue notes	notes used in jazz that are purposely performed out of tune, or that contradict the harmony
bossa nova	a Latin American dance rhythm

break	the section in a jazz piece when an instrument plays a solo, usually improvised
bridge	in jazz, the term for the B section of a 32 bar song, also called the middle eight
call and response	a device in which a solo singer is answered by a group; often the group sings the same response each time
canon	a device in which all parts perform the same music but start one after the other
cha-cha	a Latin American dance rhythm,

chord chart	the name given to the system of indicating chords by letters and numbers that is used by the rhythm section in jazz
chromaticism	the use of accidentals
circle (or cycle) of fifths	a chord progression in which successive chords are a fifth apart, C – F – B flat – E flat, etc
clave rhythm	a rhythm found in much Latin American music,

common tones	notes that stay the same when chords are altered
comping	the accompaniment provided by a keyboard player in jazz
cross-rhythm	different rhythms performed at the same time
crushed note	a short note played before a melody note
decoration	the addition of usually rapid notes added to an existing melody line
diatonic	music that is within a key structure
dissonance	notes that sound as if they don't belong together

133

dorian mode	a scale form with the following pattern

drone	performing one note continually as an accompaniment
dynamics	differences in volume
elastic scoring	a term used by Percy Grainger implying that an arrangement could be played by different combinations of instruments
enharmonics	notes that have more than one name, A sharp and B flat, for example
ensemble	a musical group
explosions	in bebop drumming, sudden drum/cymbal crashes
falsetto	a vocal effect using a high, unnatural sound
flutter tonguing	in wind instruments, playing with rapid fluctuations of the tongue
glide	to slide between notes
glissando	sliding between notes up and down the scale
head	the main part of a jazz composition, in an AABA pattern, the A section
heptatonic	a scale with seven notes, eg

honkytonk	a style of white rural 12 bar blues
hurdy-gurdy	ancient folk instrument with strings sounded by a hand driven wheel
idiophone	instrument that sounds 'by itself', eg castanet, claves
improvisation	the practice of making music up as it is performed
instrumentation	the instruments needed to perform a piece
inversion	a different version of a chord made by changing the order of the notes
iterative	repetitive
Jindyworobakism	a movement in Australian literature and music which started in the 1950s and showed Aboriginal influences
jongleur	a medieval musician
lagerphone	a percussion instrument used in Australian bush music. It is made from a broom stick covered with nailed on beer bottle tops
Magyar music	music of the Hungarian gypsies
modal jazz	jazz that uses modes, eg dorian mode, see above
orchestration	the way in which different instruments have been utilised in a piece of music
ostinato	a repetitive pattern
pantum	an Asian dance
pedal point	the use of a sustained note under a passage of music
pentatonic	music using only five notes, eg

pitch range	the notes between the highest and lowest notes in a piece
polyrhythm	the presence of conflicting time signatures at the same time
reggae	a type of Jamaican rock music
rhythm and blues	popular style of black music using the 12 bar pattern
riff	a repeated pattern, often a bass guitar part, or chord change
scat singing	using the voice to imitate instruments
serial	a style of composition developed by Schoenberg early in the 20th century in which all twelve notes of the chromatic scale are ordered and manipulated
serial techniques	the compositional methods used by serial composers, eg retrograde, inversion
shots	sudden offbeat accents played on the snare drum in bebop
slurring	connecting notes in performance
stride playing	a method of piano playing in which the left hand plays octaves on the beat and the right hand plays chords on the offbeat; the name describes the visual effect of the left hand
strophic	having verses
substitution	using an alternative chord that also fits the harmony
swing rhythm	in swing jazz is interpreted as
syncopation	when the accents in music are displaced on to normally unaccented beats
ternary form	a three part plan, ABA
timbre	the distinctive sound of each instrument
tone colour	see timbre
transpose	to move music to another pitch level
triad	a standardised ordering of three notes, eg

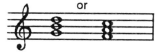

trill	rapid alternation of two adjacent notes
tritone substitution	substitution in which the substituted chord is a tritone apart from the original
32 bar song form	a standard plan used in many jazz songs in which there are four 8 bar sections, AABA
12 bar blues	a standard chord pattern used as the basis for many types of popular music, eg

12 tone music	see serial
vamping	piano style, see stride playing
vergules	the 'stems' of notes used to show rhythm in guitar parts
vibrato	small, rapid fluctuations of a note
vielle	an ancient, bowed string instrument
zydeco	a type of 12 bar blues played on piano accordion

Acknowledgements

The authors and publisher would like to thank copyright holders for permission to reproduce the following copyright material:

Music

''Denn Wie Man Sich Bettet'' from *The Rise and Fall of the City of Mahagonny* by Kurt Weill and Bertolt Brecht. Reprinted by permission of the Kurt Weill Foundation for Music.
''Down Under'' by Colin Hay and Ron Strykert, © 1981 SBK Songs Australia Pty. Ltd., PO Box C156, Cremorne Junction, NSW, 2090.
''Rhapsody in Blue'' by George Gershwin, Chappell & Intersong Music Group Australia Ltd.
''Rum and Coca Cola'' by M. Amsterdam, Jerry Sullivan and Paul Baron. Reprinted by permission of J. Albert and Son Pty. Ltd., 9 Rangers Rd, Neutral Bay, NSW, 2089.
''Skylark'' by Hoagy Carmichael and Johnny Mercer. Copyright © 1942 Edwin H. Morris & Company Inc. For Australia and New Zealand J. Albert and Son Pty. Ltd., 9 Rangers Rd, Neutral Bay, NSW, 2089. Used by permission. All rights reserved.
''Someday My Prince Will Come'' by Churchill and Morey. Reprinted by kind permission of Allans Music Australia Pty. Ltd., PO Box C156, Cremorne Junction, NSW, 2090.
''Stormy Weather'' by Harold Arlen and Ted Koehler. Reprinted by permission of J. Albert & Son Pty. Ltd., 9 Rangers Rd, Neutral Bay, NSW, 2089.
''Take Five'' by Paul Desmond. Reprinted by permission of Frankdon Music Pty. Ltd., Sydney, Australia.
''The Queen and the Soldier'' by Suzanne Vega, © Copyright 1986 AGF Music Ltd. For Australia & New Zealand: Mushroom Music Pty. Ltd.
''Tuxedo Junction'' by Buddy Feyne, Erskin Hawkins, William Johnson and Julian Dash. © Lewis Music. Reproduced by permission of Boosey & Hawkes (Australia) Pty. Ltd.
''Unsquare Dance'' by Dave Brubeck. Reprinted by permission of Frankdon Music Pty. Ltd., Sydney, Australia.

Photographs

Louis Armstrong pp. 16, 65, Glenn A. Baker Archives
Benny Goodman Orchestra p. 17, Glenn A. Baker Archives
Art Blakey p. 55, W. Patrick Hinely, Work/Play
Dave Brubeck p. 58, W. Patrick Hinely, Work/Play
Don Burrows pp. 67, 113, The Australian Jazz Magazine
Kate Ceberano cover photograph and p. 113, Fred Bray (photographer) and Kate Ceberano Productions
Tracy Chapman p. 87, Tony Mott
Ornette Coleman p. 68, W. Patrick Hinely, Work/Play
Corroboree Scenes p. 101, Steve Strike
Miles Davis p. 25, Glenn A. Baker Archives
Maynard Ferguson p. 72, W. Patrick Hinely, Work/Play
Ella Fitzgerald p. 16, Glenn A. Baker Archives
Dizzy Gillespie p. 24, Jane March
Graeme Bell All Stars p. 112, The Australian Jazz Magazine
Percy Grainger p. 106, The Grainger Museum, University of Melbourne